To:

Aunt Beth & Uncle John

From: Sarah Christmas 2013

Once Upon a Time

Once Upon a Time

Recipes and Recollections From a River City

The Junior League of Evansville, Indiana

Once Upon a Time

Recipes and Recollections From a River City

The Junior League of Evansville, Inc.
123 NW 4th Street
Suite 422
Evansville, Indiana 47708
812-423-9127

Copyright © 2003 by
The Junior League of Evansville, Inc.

ISBN: 0-9729885-0-5
Library of Congress Number: 2003103514

Edited, Designed and Manufactured by
Favorite Recipes® Press

FRP

P.O. Box 305142
Nashville, Tennessee 37230
800-358-0560

Book Design: Jim Scott
Art Director: Steve Newman
Project Editor: Ginger Dawson

Manufactured in the United States of America

First Printing: 2003

10,000 copies

About the Artist— Peg Annakin

This Evansville native has been called many things, the more printable being Peggy Ann and Peggy Sue, but really just prefers to be called Peg. A brief history of Peg (as she is now known) will reveal that she studied at a local college, married her high school sweetheart, and is the mother of two incredibly cute children.

This whimsical artist enjoys reproducing vintage artwork, and her love of roosters inspired her to create a hand-painted cocktail bag business she calls "Cocktail-Doodle-Doo!" Her artistic turn-ons include Matisse, the entire state of California, and the 3 D's: dress-up, decorating, and doodling. She is also a proud member of the Junior League of Evansville.

Cookbook Development Committee

Chairman

Kirsten Wagmeister

The Junior League of Evansville is an organization of women committed to promoting voluntarism, developing the potential of women, and improving the community through the effective action and leadership of trained volunteers. Our purpose is exclusively educational and charitable.

Art and Design

Peg Annakin, *Chairman*
Lea Alcock
Karen Meacham
Lori Moore
Michelle Peterlin

Non-Recipe Text

Francesca Brougham,
    Chairman
Allison Comstock
Janet Keller
Wendy McCormick
Monica Shakun
Melissa Wagner

Marketing

Melissa Toney Robinson,
    Chairman
Suzette Broshears
Andi Miller
Jane Royalty

Recipes

Michele Kinkel, *Chairman*
Kristie Alexander
Cindy Behrens
Allison Hemmerlein
Bethany Hunt
Allison Lueking
Joelle Lynch
Vicki Rohleder
Amy Will
Diana Zausch

Special Thanks

Gray Photography
University of Evansville
    Department of Theatre
Karen Meacham
Special Collections,
    Willard Library
Evansville Museum of Arts,
    History and Science
West Side Nut Club
Evansville Living Magazine

Tucker Publishing Group
Todd and Kristen Tucker
Sara Ann Corrigan
Colormax
Colonial Home and
    Garden Center
The Alexander Family
The Annakin Family
The Brougham Family
The Hemmerlein Family
The Kinkel Family

The McCormick-Fleming
    Family
The Meacham Family
The Moser Family
The Peterlin Family
The Rohleder Family
The Shakun Family
The Wagmeister Family
Luise F. Schnakenburg
Deaconess Hospital

Contents

Foreword

The Evansville of my childhood was void of nationally known fast food restaurants. On those rare occasions when families went out to eat, the cuisine most likely would have been fried catfish (fiddlers) or barbeque at Mac's, Wolfe's, or Marx's. Although Evansville now abounds with restaurants, offering a variety of food choices, few date back fifty years to the Evansville of my youth.

The practice of frequently eating outside the home is a relatively new phenomenon. What once was a rare treat for most families is now a common occurrence. As a consequence, few families hand down favorite recipes, or secret recipes, from one generation to the next. One often hears, "Remember grandmother's oyster dressing? I wish I knew how to make it." "Remember those coconut cream pies Aunt Anna used to bake? I wish I had her recipe."

The Evansville in which I was a boy was a city of home cooking. Surrounded by farms, it was a city of vegetables (corn, green beans, tomatoes, radishes, carrots, potatoes, green onions), fruits (apples, pears, cantaloupe, watermelon, strawberries, blackberries), meats (beef, pork, lamb), fresh eggs, and fresh milk. It was a city in which, for the most part, men worked away from the home and women worked at home raising children and cooking, often three meals a day. Not every meal would have drawn a smile from Betty Crocker, or later Martha Stewart, but often, and particularly on special occasions, grandmothers, mothers, and daughters laid a table "fit for a king." Sunday dinners were often special occasions. Before leaving for church, the women of the house would brown a beef roast in a large black iron pot and surround it with carrots, potatoes, and onions. A top was placed on the pot, and the pot was placed in the oven on low heat, where it would slowly cook while the family attended church. When one walked into the house after church, the aroma of the cooking food would have filled the house, and one's first whiff carried promise of what was to come. It was a family dinner, often with relatives, which the adults stretched into hours with conversation over coffee and dessert.

During the winter, desserts were cakes, or pies that could be made with store-bought filling or from fruits that had been canned and "put up" for the winter. During the summers, however, the desserts were pies made from fresh apples or peaches, or cobblers made from fresh blackberries. An additional summer treat was having the dessert served with homemade ice cream, cranked by hand and packed in the bucket, with salted ice, to harden. I never heard anyone in Evansville use the word "calorie." After the meal, a white tablecloth was pulled over the food on the table, and in the evening, if anyone was hungry, they could eat from what was left over.

Through the mystery of the senses, the smell of certain foods or the taste of certain flavors bring instantly to my memory faces that have long faded and names almost forgotten, which I immediately associate with meals shared or special recipes. For some, this book will become a frigate on which one can sail into the past to large kitchens with pots boiling, ovens baking, indescribable aromas, and tables laden with the magic of well-prepared food, some from secret recipes revealed herein for the very first time.

James C. Coomer

James C. Coomer was born and grew up in Evansville. He is Emeritus Professor of Political Science at Mercer University, where he was Senior Vice President for Academic Affairs. He is the author of several books, including An Indiana Childhood and Other Stories, *his first collection of short stories. He presently lives and writes in Norcross, Georgia.*

Great
Beginnings

In a League of Our Own

Who we are... Throughout the past 75 years, the Junior League of Evansville, Inc. (JLE) has touched many lives throughout the Evansville area. We were established in 1926 by 20 insightful women who, *once upon a time*, sought to promote voluntarism and cultural development in our community. Today, more than 400 area women, representing a cross section of professions and age groups, are active or sustaining members.

What we do... Our mission, "to improve communities though the effective action and leadership of trained volunteers," serves as the foundation for everything we do. Our focus areas of women, children, and education serve as a compass to guide us in our efforts to make Evansville and the surrounding area a better place to live. We accomplish this by dedicating volunteers and funding to new and existing projects.

Our very first project in 1926 was support for the Babies Milk Fund Association, which later became the Public Health Nursing Association. Through the years, the welfare of children continued to be an important goal of JLE, as seen by our development and support of such projects as the Hands On Discovery Children's Museum, the Little Lambs prenatal incentive program, a handicapped-accessible playground, and the creation of ARK Crisis Prevention Nursery.

The legacy continues... Our other interests have run the gamut of community needs. We've undertaken cultural development, historical preservation, environmental issues, and health concerns. However, it is impossible to list all the projects we've completed or to imagine the vast number of lives we've touched since our inception in 1926. New projects are currently in development as we continue to monitor our community needs and the ways in which we can fulfill those needs. As our world changes, so must we. And with that in mind, we look to the future with optimism, flexibility, and the satisfaction that comes from doing our best.

By purchasing this cookbook, you've provided us with a means to continue our efforts in the local area. Thank you for helping us make a difference.

Appetizers and Beverages

Crispy Smoked Trout and Crab Cakes with Cucumber Dill Tartar Sauce

Evansville Country Club, Executive Chef Kenneth Thompson, C.S.C.

Tartar Sauce

1 cucumber, peeled, chopped	1 teaspoon chopped fresh dill weed
1/2 cup plain yogurt	1/8 teaspoon cayenne pepper
1/2 cup sour cream	Salt and freshly ground black pepper
Juice of 1 lemon	to taste
2 teaspoons minced garlic	

Trout and Crab Cakes

3/4 cup mayonnaise	1 tablespoon Worcestershire sauce
1/2 small red onion, minced, sautéed	1 teaspoon dry mustard
1/4 cup minced fresh chives	1/2 cup flaked smoked trout
1 egg	1/2 cup lump crab meat
1 tablespoon Old Bay seasoning	3 1/2 cups fresh bread crumbs
1 tablespoon lemon juice	Vegetable oil for frying

13

For the tartar sauce, combine the cucumber, yogurt, sour cream, lemon juice, garlic, dill weed and cayenne pepper in a small bowl. Season with salt and black pepper. (May prepare the sauce up to 2 days in advance. Chill, covered, until ready to use.)

For the trout and crab cakes, combine the mayonnaise, onion, chives, egg, Old Bay seasoning, lemon juice, Worcestershire sauce and dry mustard in a medium bowl with a wire whisk until well mixed. Stir in the trout and crab meat with a rubber spatula. Add 1/2 cup of the bread crumbs and mix well.

Place the remaining 3 cups bread crumbs in a bowl. Divide the trout mixture into 1/3 cup (3-ounce) portions. Roll each portion in the bread crumbs until evenly coated, then form into a flat 1/4-inch-thick disk or cake.

Pour the oil into a straight-sided sauté pan or deep fryer to a 2-inch depth. Heat to 300 degrees. Fry the cakes for 3 to 4 minutes or until brown on both sides. Drain on paper towels. Serve immediately with the Tartar Sauce. *Yield: 4 to 6 servings.*

NOTE: THE FRIED CAKES MAY ALSO BE SERVED ON A BED OF MIXED GREENS THAT HAVE BEEN TOSSED WITH THOUSAND ISLAND SALAD DRESSING, THINLY SLICED RED ONION, SHREDDED CARROTS, CROUTONS, AND CRISP BACON PIECES.

Shrimp Rockefeller Ricotta Torte

Rolling Hills Country Club, Chef Michael Dell, C.E.C.

1 leek, white part and 1 inch of green part only, split lengthwise
1 carrot, cut into thin wide strips
2 tablespoons chopped shallots
1 teaspoon chopped garlic
1 tablespoon butter
¹/₂ pound jumbo shrimp, peeled, deveined and cut into quarters
4 ounces fresh spinach leaves

¹/₂ cup bacon bits
2 tablespoons sambuca
6 ounces ricotta cheese
6 ounces feta cheese
4 eggs, beaten
1 teaspoon chopped fresh tarragon
1 teaspoon chopped fresh thyme
¹/₂ cup Italian-style bread crumbs
3 tablespoons grated Parmesan cheese

Blanch the leek and carrot strips in a pot of boiling salted water for 2 minutes. Drain and pat dry. Starting at the center, line the bottom and sides of a buttered 1¹/₂-quart deep baking dish with the leek and carrot strips. Alternate the leek and carrot strips to resemble the spokes of a wheel, letting the ends of the strips hang over the edge of the dish; set aside.

Cook the shallots and garlic in the butter in a covered sauté pan over low heat until soft but not brown. Add the shrimp. Cook until the shrimp turn pink. Stir in the spinach and bacon. Cook until the spinach is wilted. Add the sambuca to the pan, stirring to deglaze. Remove to a baking sheet, spreading out in a thin layer to cool.

Combine the ricotta cheese, feta cheese, eggs, tarragon, thyme and cooled shrimp mixture in a bowl until well mixed. Stir in the bread crumbs and Parmesan cheese. Spoon into the prepared baking dish, packing down firmly. Fold the ends of the leek and carrot strips over the top of the shrimp mixture, adding more strips if necessary to cover completely. Cover the dish with foil, tenting it so the foil does not touch the surface of the torte.

Place the baking dish in a larger baking pan. Add enough water to the baking pan to reach halfway up the sides of the baking dish. Bake at 350 degrees for 1¹/₄ hours. Remove from the oven and let stand for 15 minutes. Invert onto a serving dish. Cut into wedges and serve with crackers or toast points. *Yield: 6 to 8 first-course or 12 buffet servings.*

NOTE: MAY ALSO BE BAKED IN A 9-INCH SPRINGFORM PAN IN THE WATER BATH. PRESS HEAVY-DUTY FOIL TIGHTLY OVER THE BOTTOM AND SIDE OF THE PAN TO PREVENT LEAKAGE.

New Orleans Barbecued Shrimp

4 pounds unpeeled large shrimp, or
6 pounds large shrimp with heads
$^{1}/_{2}$ cup (1 stick) butter
$^{1}/_{2}$ cup olive oil
$^{1}/_{4}$ cup chili sauce
$^{1}/_{4}$ cup Worcestershire sauce
2 lemons, sliced
4 garlic cloves, chopped

2 tablespoons Creole seasoning
2 tablespoons lemon juice
1 tablespoon chopped parsley
1 teaspoon paprika
1 teaspoon oregano
1 teaspoon cayenne pepper
$^{1}/_{2}$ teaspoon hot red pepper sauce
French bread

Spread the shrimp in a shallow foil-lined broiler pan; set aside.

Heat the butter, olive oil, chili sauce, Worcestershire sauce, lemons, garlic, Creole seasoning, lemon juice, parsley, paprika, oregano, cayenne pepper and pepper sauce in a saucepan over low heat until the butter is melted, stirring frequently. Pour over the shrimp; cover. Chill for 2 hours, turning the shrimp every 30 minutes.

Uncover the shrimp. Bake at 400 degrees for 20 minutes or until the shrimp turn pink, turning once. Serve with French bread to sop up the excess sauce. *Yield: 16 to 18 servings.*

Polynesian Pops

1 bunch (about 7) ripe bananas
$^{1}/_{4}$ cup curry powder

4 ounces very thinly sliced prosciutto
Mango chutney

Cut the bananas crosswise into quarters, making four 4-inch pieces of each slice. Place the curry powder in a sealable plastic bag. Add the banana slices and seal the bag. Shake until all the bananas are lightly coated.

Cut each prosciutto slice into quarters, making four 4-inch pieces of each slice. Wrap a prosciutto piece around the edge of each coated banana slice, securing in place with a wooden pick. Place on a baking sheet.

Broil for 8 minutes or until bubbly, turning once. Serve warm with chutney. *Yield: 30 servings.*

When considering the number of appetizers to serve at your next party, keep in mind the type of appetizers on the menu (hearty or light) and whether a meal will follow. If dinner will also be served, allow four to five appetizers per guest. If the appetizers are to take the place of a meal, allow eight to nine appetizers per guest.

Pork Satay with Peanut Sauce

Pork

1 pound pork tenderloin, cut into $^1/_4 \times 2$-inch strips

$^3/_4$ cup canned coconut milk

2 teaspoons brown sugar

1 teaspoon salt

1 teaspoon minced fresh cilantro

1 teaspoon cumin

1 teaspoon turmeric

Peanut Sauce

$1^1/_4$ cups canned coconut milk

2 teaspoons red curry paste

$^1/_2$ cup chunky peanut butter

2 tablespoons sugar

1 teaspoon salt

$^1/_2$ teaspoon lemon juice

For the pork, place the tenderloin strips in a 1-gallon sealable plastic bag. Add the coconut milk, brown sugar, salt, cilantro, cumin and turmeric. Seal the bag and knead it until all the ingredients are well mixed. Marinate in the refrigerator for 8 to 12 hours.

For the peanut sauce, heat half the coconut milk with the curry paste in a saucepan over low heat for 3 minutes, stirring constantly. Stir in the peanut butter, sugar, salt, lemon juice and remaining coconut milk. Bring to a simmer. Simmer gently for 20 to 30 minutes or until thickened, stirring occasionally. Remove to a serving bowl; set aside.

Soak bamboo skewers in water for 20 minutes to 2 hours. Remove the pork from the marinade; discard the marinade. Thread the pork strips onto the soaked skewers. Grill for 12 to 15 minutes or until cooked through, turning frequently. Serve with the Peanut Sauce for dipping. *Yield: 8 servings.*

NOTE: RED CURRY PASTE CAN BE FOUND IN ASIAN GROCERY STORES.

Black Bean Tart with Chili Crust

Crust

1¼ cups flour
1 teaspoon cumin
1 teaspoon chili powder
1 teaspoon paprika
½ teaspoon salt

½ cup (1 stick) unsalted
butter or margarine,
chilled, cut into pieces
2 tablespoons ice water

Filling

1 (10-ounce) package frozen
corn, thawed
1 tablespoon vegetable oil
Salt and pepper to taste
2 cups canned black beans,
rinsed, drained
1½ cups (6 ounces) shredded
Monterey Jack cheese

1 red bell pepper, chopped
(about 1 cup)
½ cup cilantro sprigs,
chopped
½ cup chopped scallions
(about 2)

For the crust, combine the flour, cumin, chili powder, paprika and salt
in a bowl. Cut in the butter until crumbly. Add the water 1 tablespoon
at a time, mixing with a fork until the mixture begins to form a ball.
Press the dough evenly onto the bottom and side of a 10-inch fluted
tart pan with a removable bottom. Chill for 15 minutes or until firm.
Line the pastry shell with foil and fill with uncooked rice or pie
weights. Bake at 350 degrees for 8 to 10 minutes. Remove the foil
and rice carefully. Continue baking the pastry for 10 minutes or until
golden brown. Cool in the pan on a wire rack. (May prepare the crust
up to 1 day in advance. Let stand at room temperature loosely
covered with plastic wrap.)

    For the filling, sauté the corn in the oil in a skillet over medium-
high heat for about 2 minutes. Cool completely; season with salt and
pepper. Combine the corn, beans, cheese, bell pepper, cilantro and
scallions in a large bowl. Season with salt and pepper. Spoon into
the crust, pressing gently. Bake at 350 degrees for 20 minutes or
until heated through and the cheese is melted. Cool in the pan for
15 minutes. Remove the rim from the pan and cool completely. Serve
at room temperature with Lime Sour Cream (at right).
Yield: 8 to 10 servings.

Lime Sour Cream

*Serve a dollop of this lively
sauce with the Black Bean
Tart with Chili Crust.*

1 cup sour cream
2 teaspoons fresh lime juice
Salt and pepper to taste

*Whisk the sour cream and lime
juice in a bowl. Season with salt
and pepper. Chill, covered, up
to 1 day in advance. Great
with fajitas and enchiladas, too!*

17

Kazootie Pie

1 (2-crust) pie pastry
2¼ cups (9 ounces) shredded
fontina cheese

2 cups shredded zucchini

Line a 9-inch pie plate with ½ of the pastry. Layer 1 cup of the cheese and ½ of the zucchini in the pastry shell. Repeat the layers, ending with the remaining ¼ cup cheese. Cut the remaining pastry into strips. Arrange lattice-fashion over the pie.

Bake at 500 degrees for 15 minutes. Reduce the oven temperature to 375 degrees. Bake for 20 minutes. Serve warm. *Yield: 8 to 10 servings.*

Corn Tartlets

Filling

1 cup cooked corn, well drained
2 scallions, minced
2 tablespoons finely chopped
red bell pepper
2 tablespoons chopped fresh basil

¼ cup olive oil
1 tablespoon hot chili oil
Salt and freshly ground black pepper
to taste

Pastry

6 tablespoons butter, softened
3 ounces cream cheese, softened
1 cup flour

½ cup yellow cornmeal
⅛ teaspoon salt

For the filling, toss the corn, scallions, bell pepper, basil, olive oil and chili oil in a bowl. Season with salt and black pepper. Marinate, covered, in the refrigerator for 3 to 4 hours.

For the pastry, cream the butter and cream cheese in a mixing bowl with an electric mixer. Combine the flour, cornmeal and salt in another bowl. Mix into the butter mixture gradually. Knead lightly to form a pastry dough. Roll the dough into 1-inch balls. Press each ball into a greased tartlet tin or miniature muffin cup, indenting the center with your thumb. Bake at 350 degrees for 15 to 20 minutes. Remove the tartlet shells from the oven before they turn golden brown. Do not overbake. Cool completely in the tins.

Fill the cooled tartlet shells with the corn mixture. *Yield: 2 dozen tartlets.*

Spinach Pastries

¹/₃ cup chopped onion
2 tablespoons unsalted butter
1 (10-ounce) package frozen chopped
  spinach, thawed, drained
10 ounces ricotta cheese
4 ounces feta cheese, crumbled

2 eggs, beaten
¹/₂ teaspoon salt
¹/₄ teaspoon pepper
¹/₂ cup (1 stick) unsalted butter, melted
1 (16-ounce) package frozen phyllo
  dough, thawed

Sauté the onion in 2 tablespoons butter in a skillet. Add the spinach. Sauté for 2 to 3 minutes. Stir in the ricotta cheese, feta cheese, eggs, salt and pepper; set aside.

Lightly brush the bottom of a 9×13-inch pan with some of the melted butter. Layer 6 sheets of phyllo dough in the pan, brushing each sheet liberally with melted butter. Spread the spinach mixture evenly over the phyllo in the pan. Layer at least 6 sheets of the remaining phyllo dough over the spinach mixture, brushing each sheet liberally with melted butter. Tuck any excess phyllo dough down the sides of the pan with a spatula. With the tip of a sharp knife, cut through the top layers of phyllo into serving-size portions.

Bake at 350 degrees for 45 minutes. Let stand for 10 minutes before cutting all the way through and serving. *Yield: 8 to 10 servings.*

NOTE: TO PREVENT THE PHYLLO DOUGH FROM DRYING OUT WHILE ASSEMBLING THIS DISH, PLACE IT BETWEEN TWO CLEAN, DAMP DISH TOWELS. AFTER REMOVING A SHEET FROM THE STACK, KEEP THE REST COVERED. IF SOME SHEETS BREAK OR TEAR, DON'T DESPAIR—BAKED PHYLLO IS WONDERFULLY FLAKY AND CRISP AND NO ONE WILL NOTICE.

VARIATION: FOR MEAT PASTRIES, SUBSTITUTE **1** POUND GROUND BEEF FOR THE SPINACH AND **¹/₂** TEASPOON GARLIC SALT FOR THE SALT. BROWN THE GROUND BEEF WITH THE ONION, STIRRING UNTIL CRUMBLY; DRAIN. STIR IN **2** TABLESPOONS TOMATO PASTE AND **1** ADDITIONAL EGG, BEATEN, WITH THE CHEESES.

Classic Bruschetta

Hors d'oeuvre is a French term meaning "(dishes) outside the work (meal)."

8 Roma tomatoes, seeded, chopped
2 cups julienned fresh basil, chopped
3 tablespoons olive oil
1 tablespoon balsamic vinegar

1 teaspoon salt
1 teaspoon minced garlic
1 loaf French bread, sliced
Olive oil for brushing

Combine the tomatoes, basil, 3 tablespoons olive oil, the vinegar, salt and garlic in a medium bowl. Let stand, covered, at room temperature for at least 4 hours. Brush 1 side of each French bread slice with olive oil. Place oil side up on a baking sheet. Bake in a 350-degree oven for 5 minutes or until golden brown. Cool completely. Spoon the tomato mixture onto the French bread slices and serve. *Yield: 8 to 10 servings.*

Artichoke Bruschetta

1 (6-ounce) jar marinated artichoke hearts, drained, patted dry, chopped
$1/2$ cup (2 ounces) grated Romano cheese
$1/3$ cup finely chopped red onion

5 to 6 tablespoons mayonnaise
16 French bread slices, about $1/3$ inch thick

Combine the artichoke hearts, cheese and onion in a bowl and mix well. Stir in enough of the mayonnaise to form a thick spread. Top the bread slices with the artichoke spread. Arrange on a baking sheet.

Broil for about 2 minutes or until the spread is heated through and begins to brown. *Yield: 8 servings.*

Roasted Red Pepper Bruschetta

1 (16-ounce) loaf French bread,
cut into 24 slices
1 medium red onion, coarsely chopped
1 teaspoon sugar
2 tablespoons olive oil

24 small fresh basil leaves
1 (7-ounce) jar roasted red peppers,
drained, cut into thin strips
3 ounces goat cheese, crumbled

Place the bread slices on baking sheets. Broil 6 inches from the heat source for 1 minute on each side or until golden brown; set aside.

Cook the onion and sugar in the olive oil in a large skillet over medium-low heat for 25 minutes, stirring occasionally. Cool completely.

Top the toasted bread slices with the onion mixture, basil leaves and red pepper strips. Sprinkle with the cheese. Broil for 1 minute or until the cheese melts. Serve immediately. *Yield: 2 dozen bruschetta.*

Tomato Basil Focaccia

1 (10-ounce) can refrigerator pizza crust
2 cups (8 ounces) shredded mozzarella,
cheese, divided
4 plum tomatoes, thinly sliced
1 ounce fresh Parmesan cheese, grated

$^2/_3$ cup mayonnaise
2 tablespoons snipped fresh basil, or
2 teaspoons dried basil
1 garlic clove, chopped

Roll out the pizza dough on a greased baking sheet. Sprinkle with 1 cup of the mozzarella cheese. Arrange the tomatoes in a single layer over the cheese; set aside.

Combine the remaining 1 cup mozzarella cheese, the Parmesan cheese, mayonnaise, basil and garlic in a small bowl and mix well. Spoon over the tomatoes, spreading evenly.

Bake at 375 degrees for 15 to 20 minutes. Cut into pieces. Serve warm. *Yield: 20 servings.*

Italian Flag Torta

8 ounces cream cheese, softened
11 ounces prepared pesto (pour off oil and stir before measuring)
Salt and black pepper to taste
8 ounces cream cheese, softened
2 ounces goat cheese, softened
$^1/_2$ cup (2 ounces) grated Parmesan cheese

1 teaspoon minced garlic
8 ounces cream cheese, softened
1 (12-ounce) jar roasted red peppers, well drained
$1^1/_2$ to 2 (8-ounce) jars sun-dried tomatoes, well drained, chopped

Brush the bottom and side of a 9-inch springform pan with canola oil. Line the pan with two 30-inch-long pieces of plastic wrap, crisscrossing them to completely cover the inside. Let the excess plastic wrap hang over the pan's edge; set aside.

Beat 8 ounces cream cheese in a bowl until smooth. Add the pesto and blend well. Season with salt and black pepper. Spread over the bottom of the prepared pan.

Combine 8 ounces cream cheese, the goat cheese, Parmesan cheese and garlic in a bowl. Spread over the pesto layer. Refrigerate until chilled.

Beat 8 ounces cream cheese in a bowl until smooth. Place $^3/_4$ cup of the red peppers in a food processor and process until almost puréed (small red pepper pieces will be visible). Add to the cream cheese and mix just until combined. Spread over the goat cheese layer. Cover the top of the torta with the plastic wrap overhang. Refrigerate for at least 8 hours. (May be prepared up to 2 days in advance.)

Uncover the torta and remove the side of the pan. Invert onto a serving platter and remove the plastic wrap and bottom of the pan. Top with the sun-dried tomatoes. Garnish with fresh basil sprigs. Serve with crackers and/or French bread. *Yield: 15 to 20 servings.*

Rosemary Bean Dip with Garlic Pita Crisps

Not your average bean dip!

1 (15-ounce) can cannellini beans, drained
8 oil-pack sun-dried tomatoes, drained
1 garlic clove, chopped
1 tablespoon chopped fresh rosemary
¹/₂ cup water

¹/₄ cup olive oil
2 tablespoons red wine vinegar
Salt and pepper to taste
Garlic Pita Crisps (below)

Combine the beans, sun-dried tomatoes, garlic, rosemary, water, olive oil and vinegar in a food processor and process until smooth. Stir in additional water 1 tablespoon at a time, if necessary, to achieve the desired consistency. Season with salt and pepper. Chill, covered, for 30 minutes. Serve with Garlic Pita Crisps. *Yield: 16 servings.*

Garlic Pita Crisps

5 pita breads, split horizontally
³/₄ cup olive oil

Garlic salt to taste
Paprika to taste

Cut each pita bread half into 4 wedges with kitchen scissors or a serrated knife. Arrange the pita wedges cut sides up in a single layer on a baking sheet. Brush with the olive oil. Season with garlic salt and paprika.

Bake at 350 degrees for 15 minutes or until crisp and golden brown. Serve warm or at room temperature. *Yield: 40 crisps.*

Feisty Artichoke Spread

1 (14-ounce) can artichoke hearts, drained
¾ cup (3 ounces) freshly grated Parmesan cheese
3 ounces cream cheese

¼ cup mayonnaise
1 tablespoon Worcestershire sauce
1 garlic clove, minced
½ teaspoon hot red pepper sauce
¼ teaspoon black pepper

Combine the arichoke hearts, Parmesan cheese, cream cheese, mayonnaise, Worcestershire sauce, garlic, pepper sauce and black pepper in a blender or food processor and pulse until finely chopped. Spoon into an 8-inch baking dish. Bake at 350 degrees for 30 minutes.
Yield: 10 to 12 servings.

Lobster Artichoke Dip

Deliciously decadent!

16 ounces cream cheese, softened
2 cups mayonnaise
12 ounces frozen canned lobster, thawed, drained
1 (14-ounce) can artichoke hearts, drained, chopped

1½ cups (6 ounces) grated Parmesan cheese
⅔ cup chopped onion

Blend the cream cheese and mayonnaise in a large bowl until smooth. Shred the lobster with your fingers, discarding any cartilage. Add the lobster, artichoke hearts, Parmesan cheese and onion to the mayonnaise mixture and mix well. Spoon into a 2-quart baking dish. Bake at 375 degrees for 30 to 40 minutes or until bubbly and heated through. Serve with crackers and bagel chips. *Yield: 14 to 16 servings.*

NOTE: MAY SUBSTITUTE **12** OUNCES IMITATION CRAB MEAT OR CANNED CRAB MEAT, DRAINED, FOR THE FROZEN CANNED LOBSTER. WHILE FROZEN LOBSTER IS EXPENSIVE, IT REALLY MAKES THIS DISH OUTSTANDING.

Baked Broccoli Cheese Spread

8 ounces sour cream
8 ounces cream cheese, softened
1 envelope ranch dip mix
2 cups (8 ounces) shredded sharp
Cheddar cheese

1 (10-ounce) package frozen chopped
broccoli, thawed, drained
$^1/_2$ cup (2 ounces) shredded sharp
Cheddar cheese

Beat the sour cream, cream cheese and dip mix in a mixing bowl at low speed. Fold in 2 cups Cheddar cheese and the broccoli. Spoon into a 1-quart baking dish.

Bake at 350 degrees for 15 minutes. Sprinkle with $^1/_2$ cup Cheddar cheese. Bake for 5 minutes or until the cheese is melted. Serve with crackers. *Yield*: 16 *servings*.

Mango Brie

$^1/_2$ (17-ounce) package frozen puff pastry
(1 sheet)
1 (1-pound) wheel Brie cheese,
rind removed

1 cup mango chutney
1 egg white, lightly beaten

Thaw the puff pastry sheet at room temperature for 20 to 30 minutes. Unfold and place in an 8-inch baking dish lightly coated with nonstick cooking spray. Place the cheese in the center of the pastry. Spread the chutney over the top of the cheese. Fold the pastry up and over the cheese until completely encased. Brush with the egg white.

Bake at 400 degrees for 15 to 20 minutes or until golden brown. Serve with crackers. *Yield*: 10 *to* 12 *servings*.

Portobello Mushroom Spread

1 (6-ounce) package portobello mushrooms, coarsely chopped
2 garlic cloves, coarsely chopped
2 sprigs of fresh rosemary, leaves removed
2 tablespoons olive oil
Kosher salt to taste
French bread slices

Sauté the mushrooms, garlic and rosemary in the olive oil in a skillet until tender and fragrant. Season with salt. Serve over bread slices with Brie cheese and red wine. *Yield: 16 servings.*

Sausage and Mushroom Dip

1 pound bulk pork sausage
1 small onion, chopped
1 (4-ounce) jar sliced mushrooms, drained
1 (5-ounce) can tomatoes, drained, chopped
6 ounces cream cheese

Brown the sausage with the onion and mushrooms in a skillet, stirring until the sausage is crumbly; drain well. Stir in the tomatoes and cream cheese. Spoon into a small baking dish. Bake at 300 degrees for 30 minutes or until heated through. Serve with crackers. *Yield: 10 to 12 servings.*

NOTE: MAY USE A MIXTURE OF HALF MILD AND HALF HOT BULK PORK SAUSAGE.

Garden Salsa with Tortilla Roll-Ups

6 to 8 medium tomatoes, seeded, coarsely chopped
6 to 8 jalapeño chiles, seeded, coarsely chopped
1 large white onion, chopped
12 large sprigs of fresh cilantro, chopped
3 large garlic cloves, minced
Juice of 3 limes
1 1/2 teaspoons salt
1 (15-ounce) can tomato sauce
Tortilla Roll-Ups (below)

Combine the tomatoes, jalapeño chiles, onion, cilantro, garlic, lime juice and salt in a bowl. Stir in the tomato sauce. Marinate, covered, in the refrigerator for 4 to 12 hours. Serve with Tortilla Roll-Ups. *Yield: 6 to 8 servings.*

VARIATION: FOR A SALSA MARINADE, PREPARE AS DIRECTED ABOVE OMITTING THE TOMATO SAUCE. STIR IN 2 TEASPOONS LIME ZEST, 5 TABLESPOONS WORCESTERSHIRE SAUCE AND 2 ADDITIONAL GARLIC CLOVES, MINCED. ADD FLANK STEAK AND MARINATE FOR AT LEAST 1 HOUR BEFORE COOKING FOR GREAT FAJITAS.

Tortilla Roll-Ups

1 (15-ounce) can refried beans
1 (4-ounce) can chopped green chiles
4 ounces cream cheese
2 tablespoons taco seasoning
10 flour tortillas
2 cups (8 ounces) shredded Mexican cheese blend

Combine the beans, green chiles, cream cheese and taco seasoning in a large microwave-safe bowl. Microwave until the cream cheese is soft enough to mix into the other ingredients.

Spread a thin layer of the bean mixture over each tortilla. Sprinkle with the cheese and roll up. Cut each tortilla roll-up crosswise into quarters. *Yield: 20 servings.*

Homemade Tortilla Chips

You can bake your own tortilla chips at home! Simply cut 7- or 8-inch tortillas into 8 wedges each. Arrange the wedges in a single layer on a baking sheet. Bake at 350 degrees for 5 to 10 minutes or until dry and crisp. Store in an airtight container at room temperature for up to 4 days or freeze for up to 2 weeks.

For cinnamon chips, which are a wonderful accompaniment to fruit dips, combine 1/2 cup sugar, 1 teaspoon cinnamon and 1/4 cup (1/2 stick) butter, melted. Brush over tortillas before cutting, baking and storing as directed above.

The Ultimate Spread

8 ounces cream cheese, softened
$^1/_4$ cup oil-pack sun-dried tomatoes, drained, chopped
$^1/_4$ cup chopped pecans
4 green onions, chopped
$^1/_2$ teaspoon salt
Worcestershire sauce to taste

Beat the cream cheese in a bowl until smooth. Add the sun-dried tomatoes, pecans, green onions, salt and Worcestershire sauce and mix well. Serve with crackers. *Yield: 12 servings.*

Savory Sausage-Stuffed Bread

1 pound bulk pork sausage
8 ounces cream cheese
4 ounces mushrooms, sliced
$^1/_2$ cup chopped onion
$^1/_2$ cup chopped green bell pepper
$^1/_4$ cup (1 ounce) grated Parmesan cheese
$^1/_4$ cup water
$^1/_4$ teaspoon oregano
$^1/_4$ teaspoon garlic salt
1 loaf French bread

Brown the sausage in a large skillet, stirring until crumbly; drain. Stir in the cream cheese, mushrooms, onion, bell pepper, Parmesan cheese, water, oregano and garlic salt. Cook until heated through, stirring to mix well; set aside.

Cut off the top third of the bread, slicing horizontally. Hollow out the center of the loaf. Fill with the sausage mixture and cover with the bread top. Wrap the filled loaf in foil and place on a baking sheet. Bake at 400 degrees for 10 minutes. Cut crosswise into slices to serve. *Yield: 8 servings.*

Cheese Puffs

1 (1-pound) loaf very thinly sliced white bread
8 ounces cream cheese, softened
1 egg yolk
2 tablespoons grated Parmesan cheese
1 tablespoon chopped fresh chives
1 teaspoon onion juice
1/2 teaspoon baking powder
1/8 teaspoon salt
1 tablespoon chopped fresh chives

Cut the bread slices into 1 1/2-inch rounds; set aside. Combine the cream cheese, egg yolk, cheese, 1 tablespoon chives, the onion juice, baking powder and salt in a bowl. Spread generously over the bread rounds. Sprinkle with 1 tablespoon chives. Place on a greased baking sheet.

Bake at 375 degrees for 15 minutes or until puffed and golden brown. Serve immediately. *Yield: 30 servings.*

NOTE: MAY BE PREPARED IN ADVANCE. AFTER ASSEMBLING, FREEZE THE UNBAKED CHEESE PUFFS ON A BAKING SHEET. WHEN FROZEN, STORE IN SEALABLE PLASTIC FREEZER BAGS. WHEN READY TO SERVE, BAKE THE FROZEN PUFFS ON A BAKING SHEET AS DIRECTED ABOVE.

Flax Seed Crackers

1 1/2 cups flour
1/2 cup flax seeds
1/4 cup (1/2 stick) unsalted butter, softened
1/2 teaspoon baking powder
1/2 teaspoon salt
1/2 cup evaporated skim milk

Combine the flour, flax seeds, butter, baking powder and salt in the bowl of a heavy-duty mixer fitted with the paddle attachment. Mix at low speed until the mixture is crumbly. Add the evaporated milk and mix until a dough forms. Remove the dough to a small bowl and cover with plastic wrap. Chill for 15 minutes.

Divide the dough into halves. Roll out 1 half to a 1/16-inch-thick rectangle on lightly floured parchment paper. Place on a baking sheet. Bake at 325 degrees for 20 minutes or until crisp and golden brown. Repeat with the remaining dough. Break the cooled crackers into small pieces. Store in airtight containers. *Yield: 4 servings.*

Cranberry Margaritas

³/₄ cup tequila
¹/₄ cup Triple Sec
1 cup frozen cranberry juice concentrate
3 cups crushed ice
Margarita salt or sugar to taste

Combine the tequila, Triple Sec, cranberry juice concentrate and ice in a blender and process until smooth. Moisten the rims of 2 margarita glasses with water. Dip the rims into salt or sugar to coat. Pour the margarita mixture into the glasses. Garnish with lime slices. *Yield: 2 servings.*

Chocolate Martini

1¹/₄ ounces vodka
1 ounce chocolate liqueur
¹/₄ ounce crème de cacao

Shake the vodka, liqueur and crème de cacao in a cocktail shaker. Serve over ice in a chilled martini glass. *Yield: 1 serving.*

NOTE: MAY SUBSTITUTE ¹/₄ OUNCE KAHLÚA FOR THE CRÈME DE CACAO.

Citrus Slush

2 tea bags	1 cup bourbon or rum
1 cup boiling water	$^1/_2$ (6-ounce) can frozen lemonade
1 cup sugar	concentrate
$3^1/_2$ cups cold water	1 (2-liter) bottle regular or diet lemon-
1 (6-ounce) can frozen orange juice	lime soda
concentrate	

Steep the tea bags in the boiling water in a heatproof container for at least 3 minutes. Stir in the sugar; remove the tea bags. Add the cold water, orange juice concentrate, bourbon and lemonade concentrate and mix well.

Pour into an ice cream freezer container. Freeze using the manufacturer's directions until no liquid remains and the mixture is slushy. (Due to the alcohol content, this mixture takes longer to firm up than ice cream.) Scoop the slush into glasses. Pour a desired amount of soda over the slush and mix. *Yield: 15 to 20 servings.*

NOTE: MAY BE PREPARED WITHOUT AN ICE CREAM FREEZER, THOUGH THE CONSISTENCY WILL BE HARDER. FREEZE IN A COVERED CONTAINER FOR ABOUT 24 HOURS OR UNTIL FIRM.

Long Island Tea

1 ounce sweet and sour mix	$^1/_2$ ounce tequila
$^1/_2$ ounce vodka	$^1/_2$ ounce gin
$^1/_2$ ounce Triple Sec	Cola or orange juice to taste
$^1/_2$ ounce light rum	

Combine the sweet and sour mix, vodka, Triple Sec, light rum, tequila and gin in a glass. Add a desired amount of cola and stir. *Yield: 1 serving.*

Sangria

1 cup orange juice
$^1/_2$ cup sugar
1 (750-milliliter) bottle white zinfandel
$^1/_4$ cup lime juice
$^1/_4$ cup lemon juice
1 lemon, sliced
1 lime, sliced
1 orange, sliced
1 kiwifruit, sliced
20 grapes

Combine the orange juice and sugar in a saucepan. Heat over low heat until the sugar dissolves. Pour into a 2-quart pitcher. Stir in the zinfandel, lime juice and lemon juice. Add the lemon, lime, orange, kiwifruit and grapes. Cover the pitcher tightly with plastic wrap. Chill for 4 to 12 hours to allow the fruit to absorb the flavors. Serve some of the fruit in each glass. *Yield: 8 to 12 servings.*

White Sangria

$^3/_4$ cup sugar
4 large oranges, sliced
2 cups orange juice, chilled
1 (750-milliliter) bottle white wine, chilled
1 (750-milliliter) bottle Champagne, chilled

Sprinkle the sugar over the oranges in a bowl; stir. Chill, covered, for 3 to 12 hours. Remove to a pitcher and add the orange juice, wine and Champagne. Stir and serve. *Yield: 8 to 12 servings.*

Frozen Daiquiri Punch

1 quart light rum
2 (12-ounce) cans frozen limeade concentrate
1 (2-liter) bottle lemon-lime soda

Combine the rum, limeade concentrate and soda in a bowl. Freeze in a covered container. Serve frozen in glasses topped with additional lemon-lime soda if desired. *Yield: 15 to 20 servings.*

NOTE: MAY SUBSTITUTE OTHER FLAVORS OF FROZEN CONCENTRATE FOR THE LIMEADE.

Wassail Bowl

Whole cloves
6 oranges
1 gallon apple cider
1$\frac{1}{2}$ cups lemon juice
10 (2-inch) cinnamon sticks
2 cups vodka
$\frac{1}{2}$ cup brandy

Insert cloves into the oranges, spacing them $\frac{1}{4}$ inch apart. (Use a knife to score the orange peel if the cloves are difficult to insert.) Place the oranges in a shallow baking pan. Bake at 350 degrees for 30 minutes.

Heat the cider in a large pot until bubbles form around the edge. Remove from the heat. Stir in the lemon juice, cinnamon sticks and baked oranges. Heat, covered, over very low heat for 30 minutes. Add the vodka and brandy and mix well. Pour into a punch bowl with the oranges. Serve warm. *Yield: 36 (4-ounce) servings.*

Evansville encompasses characteristics of all cities into one compact area of the Midwest. Some parts have a small-town feel, with family owned businesses, generations of families living within miles of each other, close-knit church and school communities, and neighbors who watch your back door. Other areas are fast-growing, modernly commercialized, and ever-developing with trendy restaurants, superstores, and living communities. Located on the river is a downtown full of daytime business hustle similar to a major metropolitan area, while surrounded by character, history, and a growing potential. One can't help but smile in anticipation of the dreams that are being developed.

Melissa Singer

Fruit Tea

2 cups water
4 tea bags
1 (12-ounce) can frozen orange juice concentrate
1 (12-ounce) can frozen lemonade concentrate
6 ounces pineapple juice
6 ounces apricot nectar or peach nectar
1 to 1¹⁄₂ cups sugar

Bring the water to a boil in a saucepan. Remove from the heat. Add the tea bags and steep for 5 minutes. Remove the tea bags and pour into a 1-gallon pitcher. Stir in the orange juice concentrate, lemonade concentrate, pineapple juice, apricot nectar and sugar to taste. Add enough additional water to make 1 gallon. Stir and serve. *Yield: 16 (8-ounce) servings.*

Orange Froth

1 cup milk
1 cup water
1 (6-ounce) can frozen orange juice concentrate, thawed
¹⁄₄ cup sugar
1 teaspoon vanilla extract
10 ice cubes

Combine the milk, water, orange juice concentrate, sugar, vanilla and ice cubes in a blender and process at high speed for 30 seconds or until the ice is crushed. Pour into glasses and serve. *Yield: 4 servings.*

Strawberry Punch

2 (2-quart) packets strawberry-kiwi drink mix
1 (12-ounce) can frozen pink lemonade concentrate
1 (46-ounce) can pineapple juice
2¹/₂ cups sugar
1 (2-liter) bottle ginger ale

Combine the drink mix, pink lemonade concentrate, pineapple juice and sugar in a bowl. Pour into a clean plastic 1-gallon milk jug. Add enough water to almost fill the jug, allowing enough room for expansion during freezing. Freeze the punch mixture until frozen.

Remove the punch from the freezer 4 to 5 hours before serving. Pour into a punch bowl and add the ginger ale. *Yield: 40 servings.*

Hot Chocolate Mix

*When your kids come in from the cold to enjoy a steaming cup of hot chocolate,
snip the ends off red licorice strips and use them as straws!*

1 (25-ounce) box nonfat dry milk powder
1 (1-pound) can chocolate drink mix
1 (1-pound) package confectioners' sugar
1 (1-pound) jar nondairy coffee creamer

Combine the milk powder, drink mix, confectioners' sugar and coffee creamer in a bowl. Store in an airtight container at room temperature.

For each cup of hot chocolate, combine ¹/₂ cup hot water with ¹/₂ cup hot chocolate mix; mix well. *Yield: 50 servings.*

Rise and
Shine

The Story of Evansville

Once upon a time, there was a charming expanse of land that was tucked in the bend of a mighty river. As with all great things, it wasn't long before the vast and fertile land was discovered. In 1812 Colonel Hugh McGary purchased 200 acres of this land from the government and built a small log cabin for himself. He had dreams of a community, too, for the land that would one day become Evansville, Indiana.

Evansville was actually named for Robert M. Evans, a territorial legislator who, with McGary, hoped to have this small town named as the seat of government for a new county in the young state of Indiana. Their efforts proved successful because when Vanderburgh County was formed in 1818, Evansville became the county seat. In the years to come, Evansville would create—and maintain—an industrial base bolstered by the many German immigrants who settled in the area.

Iron, steel, and woodworking companies thrived, and the city became a center for furniture manufacturing. Oil was discovered in the farmlands and is still drilled for today in limited quantities. During WWII, defense contracts dramatically increased the manufacturing workforce and nearly three-quarters of the city's employers engaged in some war-related work. Automobile, pharmaceutical, appliance, and farm equipment factories were established later. Today, Evansville boasts major hospitals, two universities, a regional airport, and the same technology that abounds in the largest of cities. It is also home to unique festivals, diverse communities, and beautiful architecture that has been lovingly restored and maintained.

Evansville is a tale that has no ending. The stories of this river city are as varied as the people who tell them. From the German heritage celebrated on the West Side to the exciting new development on the east, our community prepares for the future by honoring its past. The brick-paved streets of historic downtown Evansville speak not only of times gone by, but also of the new days to come. Each chapter in this tale brings new insight, new progress, and new possibility to the land that was once a sleepy river settlement.

Brunch and Breads

Eggs Florentine

Cafe Driftwood, Jody Limback

2 tablespoons white vinegar
1 gallon water
1 tablespoon vegetable oil
2 teaspoons chopped garlic
4 ounces fresh baby spinach, coarsely chopped
³/₄ cup heavy cream
¹/₄ cup (1 ounce) grated Parmesan cheese
Salt and pepper to taste
8 artichoke bottoms
8 eggs
8 slices French bread, toasted

Add the vinegar to the water in a pot. Bring to a simmer.

Heat the oil in a sauté pan. Add the garlic. Sauté for 1 minute. Add the spinach. Sauté for about 1 minute. Stir in the cream. Bring to a boil. Add the cheese. Cook until the sauce thickens, stirring constantly. Simmer for 2 to 3 minutes. Season with salt and pepper; set aside. Place 2 artichoke bottoms on each of 4 serving plates.

Add the eggs to the pot of simmering water. Poach for 4 to 6 minutes or until the whites are completely set and the yolks begin to thicken. Remove the eggs from the water with a slotted spoon and place 1 on each artichoke bottom. Top with the spinach sauce. Serve with the toasted French bread. *Yield: 4 servings*.

Bacon, Egg and Cheese Strata

16 slices bacon	8 eggs, beaten
2 onions, cut into halves, sliced lengthwise	4 cups milk
	1^1/$_2$ teaspoons salt
12 slices firm white bread	^{1}/$_2$ teaspoon dry mustard
8 ounces Cheddar cheese, shredded	^{1}/$_4$ teaspoon pepper

Cook the bacon in a skillet until crisp. Remove from the skillet and drain on paper towels. Crumble and set aside. Add the onions to the bacon drippings in the skillet. Sauté until translucent; drain on paper towels and set aside.

Layer the bread slices, bacon, onions and cheese ^{1}/$_2$ at a time in a greased 9×13-inch baking dish. Combine the eggs, milk, salt, dry mustard and pepper in a large bowl, stirring to blend. Pour over the layered ingredients in the baking dish. Chill, covered, for 24 hours before baking. Remove from the refrigerator 1 hour before baking.

Bake, uncovered, at 350 degrees for 45 to 50 minutes or until a knife inserted into the center comes out clean. *Yield: 12 servings.*

Sausage and Brie Breakfast Bake

1 pound bulk pork sausage	2 cups skim milk
8 slices white bread, crusts trimmed	2 cups heavy cream
1 (8-ounce) wheel Brie cheese, rind removed, cut into cubes	1 teaspoon salt
	1 teaspoon dry mustard
1 cup (4 ounces) grated Parmesan cheese	2 eggs
5 eggs	1 cup heavy cream

Brown the sausage in a skillet, stirring until crumbly; drain well and set aside.

Layer the bread slices, sausage, Brie cheese and Parmesan cheese in a greased 9×13-inch baking pan. Whisk 5 eggs, the milk, 2 cups cream, the salt and dry mustard in a bowl. Pour over the layered ingredients in the pan. Chill, covered, for 8 to 12 hours.

Remove the pan from the refrigerator. Whisk 2 eggs and 1 cup cream in a bowl. Pour over the layered ingredients.

Bake, uncovered, at 350 degrees for 50 minutes or until a knife inserted into the center comes out clean. *Yield: 8 to 10 servings.*

Wine and Cheese Strata

$1/2$ large loaf dry French bread, broken into pieces
3 tablespoons butter, melted
8 ounces Swiss cheese, shredded
4 ounces Monterey Jack cheese, shredded
1 ($1/4$-inch-thick) slice ham, coarsely chopped
9 eggs
$1^3/4$ cups milk
$1/4$ cup dry white wine or sherry
4 large green onions, minced
$1^1/2$ tablespoons Dijon mustard
$1/8$ teaspoon ground black pepper
$1/16$ teaspoon cayenne pepper
$3/4$ cup sour cream
$1/2$ cup (2 ounces) grated Parmesan cheese

Place the bread pieces in the bottom of a buttered 9×13-inch baking dish. Drizzle with the melted butter. Top with the Swiss cheese, Monterey Jack cheese and ham. Beat the eggs, milk, wine, green onions, Dijon mustard, black pepper and cayenne pepper in a bowl until foamy. Pour over the cheeses and ham. Cover the dish with foil, crimping the edges to seal tightly. Chill for 24 hours. Remove from the refrigerator at least 30 minutes before baking.

Bake, covered, at 325 degrees for 1 hour. Top with the sour cream and Parmesan cheese. Bake, uncovered, for 10 minutes or until a knife inserted into the center comes out clean.
Yield: 12 *servings*.

Rise and Shine Casserole

6 cups (1-inch) bread cubes
2 cups chopped ham
2 cups (8 ounces) shredded Swiss or
Cheddar cheese

6 eggs
2 cups milk (may use skim)
1 teaspoon dry mustard
1/4 teaspoon Worcestershire sauce

Place the bread cubes in the bottom of a 9×13-inch baking pan coated with nonstick cooking spray. Top with the ham and cheese. Whisk the eggs, milk, dry mustard and Worcestershire sauce in a bowl. Pour over the cheese. Chill, covered, for 8 to 12 hours. Remove from the refrigerator 15 minutes before baking.

Bake, covered, at 350 degrees for 35 to 40 minutes or until bubbly and a knife inserted into the center comes out clean. Let stand for 5 minutes before serving. *Yield: 12 servings.*

NOTE: MAY SUBSTITUTE **1** POUND BULK PORK SAUSAGE, COOKED AND DRAINED, OR **1** POUND BACON, CRISP-COOKED AND CRUMBLED, FOR THE HAM.

42

Ham and Cheese Quiche

1/2 cup mayonnaise
1/2 cup milk
2 eggs, beaten
2 tablespoons flour

1 1/2 cups chopped ham
8 ounces shredded Colby and Monterey
Jack cheese blend
1/2 cup sliced green onions

Combine the mayonnaise, milk, eggs and flour in a bowl and mix until blended. Stir in the ham, cheese and green onions. Pour into an 8-inch quiche pan. Bake at 350 degrees for 40 to 45 minutes or until a knife inserted into the center comes out clean. Serve warm or cold.
Yield: 6 to 8 servings.

Fancy Egg Scramble

Cheese Sauce

2 tablespoons butter
2 tablespoons flour
$^1/_2$ teaspoon salt
$^1/_8$ teaspoon pepper

2 cups milk
1 cup (4 ounces) shredded Cheddar
cheese

Eggs

1 cup chopped Canadian bacon
$^1/_4$ cup chopped green onions
3 tablespoons butter

12 eggs, beaten
1 (8-ounce) can mushrooms, drained

Topping

2$^1/_4$ cups bread crumbs
2 tablespoons butter, melted

$^1/_8$ teaspoon paprika

For the cheese sauce, melt the butter in a saucepan. Stir in the flour gradually. Add the salt and pepper. Add the milk gradually, stirring constantly. Cook until the sauce thickens, stirring constantly. Add the cheese. Cook until the cheese is melted, stirring constantly. Remove from the heat; set aside.

For the eggs, cook the Canadian bacon and green onions in the butter in a skillet until the green onions are tender. Add the eggs. Cook over low heat until scrambled and no raw egg is visible. Remove from the heat. Stir in the mushrooms and Cheese Sauce. Spoon into a greased 7×12-inch baking dish.

For the topping, combine the bread crumbs, butter and paprika in a bowl. Sprinkle over the eggs. Bake at 350 degrees for 30 minutes. Yield: 8 servings.

The highlight of my 4-H experience was taking projects to the fair. In my fifth year of the foods project, I was determined to win the purple grand-champion ribbon. Previously, I had won a blue first-place ribbon, but this was my year! I arose every morning and baked rolls. My father loved it because he got fresh rolls for breakfast. The morning of the fair, I got up extra early and baked two batches, chose the best-looking rolls, and confidently went to the fair. I was awarded a blue ribbon, and my cousin, who made one batch of rolls, won! I finally won the coveted ribbon in my tenth and final year. I learned two things: blue-ribbon rolls are delicious, and persistence is a virtue.

Karen Northern

Fresh Tomato Pie

1 unbaked (9-inch) pie shell
$^3/_4$ cup flour
$^1/_2$ teaspoon salt
$^1/_4$ teaspoon pepper
7 medium Roma tomatoes, sliced
5 green onions, sliced
$^1/_4$ cup chopped fresh basil
$^1/_2$ cup low-fat mayonnaise
1 cup (4 ounces) shredded Monterey Jack cheese

Prick the bottom and side of the pie shell with a fork. Bake at 400 degrees for 9 minutes. Cool completely. Reduce the oven temperature to 375 degrees.

Combine the flour, salt and pepper in a bowl. Dredge the tomato slices in the flour mixture. Arrange in layers in the pie shell. Sprinkle with the green onions and basil. Combine the mayonnaise and cheese in a bowl. Spread over the tomatoes. Bake at 375 degrees for 25 to 30 minutes. *Yield: 6 to 8 servings.*

German Pancake Bake

4 eggs, beaten
$^1/_2$ cup (1 stick) butter, melted
1 cup milk
1 cup flour

Combine the eggs and butter in a medium bowl. Add the milk and flour and mix well. Pour into a greased 9×13-inch baking dish. Bake at 425 degrees for 20 to 25 minutes. Serve immediately with confectioners' sugar and maple syrup. *Yield: 12 servings.*

German Pancakes

1 cup milk
4 eggs
$^1/_4$ cup (heaping) flour
1 tablespoon canola oil or bacon drippings
$^1/_2$ teaspoon salt

Combine the milk, eggs, flour, canola oil and salt in a blender and process until smooth. Heat a 10-inch skillet over high heat until very hot. Pour enough batter into the skillet to coat the bottom. Cook until brown spots begin to appear on both sides, turning once. Serve with maple syrup or spread with plain yogurt or jelly and roll up. This will make two to three 10-inch pancakes. *Yield: 2 to 3 servings.*

French Toast Soufflé

Bored with breakfast? If you're making French toast, pour a little of the egg batter into three or four small bowls. Stir a few drops of food coloring into each bowl. Use a clean paintbrush to paint designs on each bread slice before dipping it into the remaining egg batter. Cook as usual and you'll have an edible masterpiece! This is a fun activity to do with kids.

10 cups (1-inch) bread cubes (about 16 slices firm white bread)
8 ounces low-fat cream cheese, softened
8 eggs
1$\frac{1}{2}$ cups 2% milk
$\frac{2}{3}$ cup half-and-half
$\frac{1}{2}$ cup maple syrup
$\frac{1}{2}$ teaspoon vanilla extract
2 tablespoons confectioners' sugar

Place the bread cubes in the bottom of a 9×13-inch baking dish coated with nonstick cooking spray. Beat the cream cheese at medium speed in a mixing bowl until smooth. Add the eggs 1 at a time, mixing well after each addition. Add the milk, half-and-half, maple syrup and vanilla and mix until smooth. Pour over the bread. Chill, covered, for 8 to 12 hours. Remove from the refrigerator 30 minutes before baking.

Bake, uncovered, at 375 degrees for 50 minutes or until set and a knife inserted into the center comes out clean. Sprinkle the confectioners' sugar over the top. Serve with maple syrup and fresh fruit if desired. *Yield: 12 servings.*

Butterscotch Pull-Apart Bread

¾ cup chopped pecans
1 (24-count) package frozen yeast rolls
1 (3-ounce) package butterscotch instant pudding mix
¾ cup packed light brown sugar
½ cup (1 stick) butter or margarine, melted
1 teaspoon cinnamon

Spray a bundt pan with nonstick cooking spray. Sprinkle the pecans over the bottom of the pan. Layer the frozen rolls over the nuts. Sprinkle with the pudding mix. Combine the brown sugar, butter and cinnamon in a bowl. Pour over the rolls. Let rise, covered with waxed paper, at room temperature for 8 to 12 hours. (Rolls will double in bulk.)

Bake, uncovered, at 350 degrees for 25 to 30 minutes. (Cover with foil during the last 10 minutes of the baking time to prevent overbrowning.) Let stand for 10 minutes. Invert onto a serving plate. *Yield: 12 to 15 servings.*

NOTE: MAY BE MADE IN ADVANCE. ASSEMBLE THE BREAD AS DIRECTED ABOVE, COVER AND REFRIGERATE. REMOVE FROM THE REFRIGERATOR **2** HOURS BEFORE BAKING TO ALLOW THE ROLLS TO RISE.

Country Blueberry Coffee Cake

½ cup packed brown sugar
½ teaspoon cinnamon
1 (12-count) can large buttermilk biscuits
¼ cup (½ stick) butter, melted
½ cup quick-cooking oats
1½ cups fresh or frozen blueberries
¼ cup sugar
½ cup quick-cooking oats
2 tablespoons butter, cut into small pieces

Combine the brown sugar and cinnamon in a small bowl; mix well with a fork. Cut each biscuit into quarters. Dip each biscuit piece into the melted butter, then coat with the brown sugar mixture. Arrange in a single layer in a well-greased 8- or 9-inch square baking pan. Sprinkle with ½ cup oats.

Toss the blueberries with the sugar in a medium bowl to coat. Spoon over the biscuits. Sprinkle with ½ cup oats. Top with the butter pieces.

Bake at 375 degrees for 30 to 35 minutes. Cool for 20 minutes. Serve warm. *Yield: 9 servings.*

Pennsylvania Dutch Coffee Cake

1 teaspoon (heaping) baking soda
2 cups buttermilk
4 cups flour
2 cups sugar
1 teaspoon salt
$^1/_2$ cup shortening
$^3/_4$ cup chopped pecans
$^1/_2$ cup (1 stick) butter, melted
$^3/_4$ cup packed brown sugar
1 teaspoon cinnamon

Stir the baking soda into the buttermilk in a bowl; set aside.

Sift the flour, sugar and salt together in a bowl. Cut in the shortening until crumbly. Reserve $^1/_2$ cup of the flour mixture. Stir the buttermilk mixture into the remaining flour mixture.

Pour the batter into 3 greased 8-inch round cake pans. Sprinkle with the pecans. Pour the melted butter over the top. Combine the reserved flour mixture with the brown sugar and cinnamon in a bowl. Sprinkle over the coffee cakes.

Bake at 325 degrees for 25 to 30 minutes or until a wooden pick inserted into the center of each coffee cake comes out clean. Cut into wedges to serve. *Yield: 24 servings.*

NOTE: THESE COFFEE CAKES FREEZE WELL.

Sour Cream Coffee Cake

Crumbs

1 cup chopped pecans	3 tablespoons sugar
1/4 cup packed light brown sugar	1 teaspoon cinnamon

Cake

1 cup (2 sticks) butter, softened	1/2 teaspoon vanilla extract
2 cups sugar	1/4 teaspoon salt
2 eggs	2 cups flour
1 teaspoon baking powder	1 cup sour cream

For *the crumbs*, combine the pecans, brown sugar, sugar and cinnamon in a small bowl; set aside.

For *the cake*, cream the butter and sugar in the large bowl of an electric mixer fitted with the paddle attachment for about 2 minutes. Add the eggs and mix well. Add the baking powder, vanilla and salt and mix for about 1 minute. Add the flour and sour cream alternately, beginning and ending with the flour. Beat until smooth.

Spray two 8-inch fluted tart pans with removable bottoms with nonstick cooking spray. Spread 1/4 of the batter carefully in each pan. Sprinkle each with 1/4 of the crumbs. Repeat with the remaining batter and crumbs.

Bake at 350 degrees for 40 to 50 minutes or just until the cakes test done. (Cover the tops of the cakes loosely with foil if they brown too quickly during baking. The coffee cakes may sink a bit in the center after removing from the oven.) Cool on wire racks for about 15 minutes. Carefully remove only the sides from the pans. Cool completely. Slide a knife between the coffee cakes and the pan bottoms to remove. Yield: 2 *coffee cakes* (24 *servings*).

NOTE: THESE COFFEE CAKES KEEP WELL WHEN WRAPPED SECURELY IN PLASTIC WRAP. THEY ALSO FREEZE BEAUTIFULLY.

50

Chocolate Chip Scones

2 cups flour
$^1/_3$ cup sugar
2 teaspoons baking powder
$^1/_2$ teaspoon salt
$^1/_2$ cup (1 stick) unsalted butter, cut into $^1/_2$-inch cubes
2 eggs
$^1/_4$ cup orange juice
1 teaspoon vanilla extract
$^3/_4$ cup semisweet chocolate chips
1 egg white (optional)
$^1/_2$ teaspoon water (optional)

Combine the flour, sugar, baking powder and salt in a large bowl. Cut in the butter until crumbly. Combine the eggs, orange juice and vanilla in a small bowl. Add to the flour mixture and stir just until mixed. Knead in the chocolate chips with lightly floured hands until evenly distributed in the dough.

Pat the dough out to a $^1/_2$-inch-thick round on a lightly floured surface. Cut into 8 equal-size wedges. Place on a baking sheet. Combine the egg white and water in a small bowl. Brush over the tops of the scones.

Bake at 425 degrees for 20 to 25 minutes. Remove to a wire rack. Serve warm or at room temperature. Store in an airtight container. *Yield: 8 scones.*

Lorenzo's Apple Walnut Muffins

Lorenzo's Breads and Bistro

Lorenzo's Breads and Bistro brings a little bit of European flavor to Evansville's east side. A varied assortment of breads are baked fresh daily, and their bakery cases are stocked with delicate pastries and decadent desserts. Lorenzo's is a charming respite where one can enjoy a satisfying lunch or linger over an intimate dinner.

52

$1^1/_2$ cups all-purpose flour
$2/_3$ cup packed brown sugar
$1/_2$ cup whole wheat flour
1 tablespoon baking powder
$1/_2$ teaspoon salt
$1/_2$ teaspoon cinnamon
$1^3/_4$ cups finely chopped apples
$1/_3$ cup coarsely chopped walnuts, toasted
$3/_4$ cup milk (2% or whole)
2 tablespoons vegetable oil
1 egg, lightly beaten
2 tablespoons sugar

Combine the all-purpose flour, brown sugar, whole wheat flour, baking powder, salt and cinnamon in a medium bowl and mix well. Add the apples and walnuts and toss gently to coat. Make a well in the center of the dry ingredients. Combine the milk, oil and egg in a bowl and mix well. Pour into the well and stir just until mixed (the dough will be sticky).

Fill jumbo-size muffin cups coated with nonstick cooking spray or lined with paper $2/_3$ full. Sprinkle with the sugar. Bake at 350 degrees for 20 minutes or until the muffins test done. Remove to a wire rack to cool. *Yield: 10 jumbo muffins.*

Banana Bread

¹/₂ cup shortening	1 teaspoon baking soda
³/₄ cup sugar	1 teaspoon cinnamon
1 egg	¹/₂ teaspoon salt
4 teaspoons lemon juice	¹/₄ teaspoon nutmeg
2 cups flour	1 cup mashed bananas (2 to 3 large)

Cream the shortening and sugar in a mixing bowl with an electric mixer until light and fluffy. Beat in the egg and lemon juice. Sift the flour, baking soda, cinnamon, salt and nutmeg together in a bowl. Fold into the egg mixture and mix well. Stir in the bananas. Pour into a lightly greased 5×9-inch loaf pan or 3 greased miniature loaf pans. Bake at 350 degrees for 60 to 70 minutes (30 to 40 minutes for the miniature loaves) or until a wooden pick inserted into the center comes out clean. Cool in the pan for 10 minutes. Remove to a wire rack to cool completely. Serve with cream cheese or flavored butter. *Yield: 1 large loaf or 3 miniature loaves.*

Beer Bread

3 cups self-rising flour	3 tablespoons sugar
1 (12-ounce) can beer	Butter, melted

Combine the flour, beer and sugar in a bowl and mix well. Pour into a greased loaf pan. Bake at 350 degrees for 3 minutes. Reduce the oven temperature to 325 degrees. Bake for about 45 minutes or until the bread tests done. Brush the top of the bread with melted butter during baking when it splits. *Yield: 1 loaf.*

How Does Your Garden Grow?

Homegrown Favorites— A Taste of Evansville

These three local delicacies tell a story full of flavor and fun!

Do you burgoo? Burgoo is a regional name for a thick meat and vegetable soup that is ground, seasoned, and simmered for up to 24 hours. In these parts, when the heat of the summer fades into the cooler days of fall, it's time to start cooking! Autumn is celebrated in some neighborhoods with burgoo block parties, and many family reunions would be incomplete without it. There are annual burgoo fund-raisers, where you, too, can burgoo by the bowl or by the gallon. In days gone by, burgoo was once made from possum, raccoon, squirrel, or wild turkey and accompanied by whatever canned vegetable needed to be used up before the new harvest. Today, however, beef, pork, and chicken are the norm, but rumor has it that, to the east of Evansville, snapping turtle meat finds its way into the pot as well!

But do they make you smarter? Brain sandwiches are a local favorite made from smashed pork brains that are shaped into fritters, battered, and deep-fried. The famous fritters are served on a bun with pickles, onions, and other condiments. Not for the weak of heart, though—a single brain sandwich (about 4 or 5 ounces) contains more than 1,000 times the USDA recommended daily allowance of cholesterol! This is perhaps why many people eat them only once a year, usually at the Fall Festival. There are devotees of this delicacy, however, as brain sandwiches can be found on the menus of a few local taverns.

A catfish by any other name just wouldn't be the same! Fiddlers are small, whole, cornmeal-breaded, and fried young catfish. You can find fried catfish like this in many parts of the country, but only in and around Evansville are they called "fiddlers." This unusual moniker has been cause for confusion for some uninitiated newcomers who heard of "fiddler fests" and set out looking for musical entertainment! However, the story of how the fiddler got its name may contribute to the confusion. One local legend tells of the fishermen of the early 1900s who, *once upon a time*, stretched large nets across the river in hopes of catching whatever swam downstream. At the end of the day, when they pulled the nets out of the river, the dorsal fins of the young catfish quivered in the evening breeze. It is said these vibrations cast an eerie cacophony over the Ohio River that was similar to that of an orchestra tuning up before a concert—and so the name "fiddlers" was born.

Special thanks to Sara Ann Corrigan of Evansville Living for her inspiration!

Salads

Spring Greens with Vanilla Vinaigrette

$^1/_2$ vanilla bean (whole bean split lengthwise)
$^3/_4$ cup olive oil
$^1/_2$ cup white wine vinegar
Juice of $^1/_2$ lemon
2 tablespoons sugar
12 cups mixed salad greens
Stilton cheese, crumbled, to taste
Dried cranberries to taste

Scrape the seeds from the vanilla bean half with the tip of a sharp knife. (The seeds are very tiny and will resemble a paste.) Combine the vanilla bean seeds, olive oil, vinegar, lemon juice and sugar in a bowl. Chill, covered, for 8 to 12 hours.

Toss the salad greens with a desired amount of the vinaigrette. (Refrigerate the remaining vinaigrette.) Top with cheese and dried cranberries. *Yield: 8 servings.*

Savory California Walnut Sprinkles

1 cup walnuts

$^1/_2$ cup fresh white bread crumbs

1 tablespoon paprika

$^1/_4$ teaspoon cayenne pepper

$^1/_4$ teaspoon salt

Chop the walnuts in a food processor fitted with a steel blade until finely ground. Remove to a small bowl. Stir in the bread crumbs. Spread in an even layer on an ungreased baking sheet. Bake at 325 degrees for 15 minutes or until golden brown and crisp, stirring frequently. Stir in the paprika, cayenne pepper and salt. Cool completely. Sprinkle over salads or pasta.

Summer Greek Salad

1 head romaine or leaf lettuce, torn into bite-size pieces
3 plum tomatoes, seeded, cut into chunks
1 cup kalamata olives
3 to 4 ounces feta cheese, coarsely crumbled
9 tablespoons extra-virgin olive oil
3 tablespoons cider vinegar
1 tablespoon fresh lemon juice
Chopped fresh oregano or dried oregano to taste
Chopped fresh mint or dried mint to taste
Salt and freshly ground pepper to taste

Combine the lettuce, tomatoes, olives and cheese in a large bowl.

Process the olive oil, vinegar, lemon juice, oregano, mint, salt and pepper in a food processor or blender. Pour over the salad. Toss to coat with the dressing. *Yield: 6 servings.*

NOTE: INGREDIENTS LISTED ARE TRADITIONAL FOR GREEK SALADS. MAY SUBSTITUTE MIXED SALAD GREENS, SLICING TOMATOES AND BLACK OLIVES FOR THE ROMAINE, PLUM TOMATOES AND KALAMATA OLIVES.

"Oh Great Caesar" Salad

3 garlic cloves
3/4 cup mayonnaise
1 teaspoon capers
1/2 teaspoon anchovy paste
2 tablespoons freshly grated Parmesan cheese
1 tablespoon fresh lemon juice
1 teaspoon Worcestershire sauce
1 teaspoon Dijon mustard
Salt and pepper to taste
1 large head romaine, cut into bite-size pieces
1/3 cup freshly grated Parmesan cheese
Croutons

Mince the garlic in a food processor fitted with a steel blade. Add the mayonnaise, capers, anchovy paste, 2 tablespoons cheese, lemon juice, Worcestershire sauce and Dijon mustard. Process until well mixed. Season with salt and pepper.

Place the romaine in a large bowl. Add enough of the dressing to coat the leaves and toss. Add 1/3 cup cheese and croutons. Toss gently to mix. *Yield: 4 to 6 servings.*

NOTE: THIS DRESSING IS ALSO DELICIOUS SERVED WITH SALMON OR USED AS A SANDWICH SPREAD. ANCHOVY PASTE IS AVAILABLE AT ITALIAN MARKETS OR GOURMET FOOD STORES.

In 1956 the Women's Society of Christian Service at Evansville's Howell Methodist Church decided to compile a cookbook to help raise money for the church. The recording secretary of the group wrote to the First Lady of the United States to request a recipe for use in the cookbook. Not only did the First Lady respond, but her husband, the President, did, too! Mrs. Eisenhower sent her favorite recipe for Pumpkin Chiffon Pie, and President Eisenhower sent his favorite recipe for Vegetable Soup.

Luise Schnakenburg

Garden Fresh Salad with Oranges and Strawberries

1 large head Bibb lettuce, torn into pieces
1 large head red leaf lettuce, torn into pieces
1 medium Bermuda onion, sliced into rings
$1/3$ cup vegetable oil
$1/3$ cup fresh orange juice
3 tablespoons red wine vinegar
2 tablespoons sugar
2 tablespoons Italian salad dressing mix
$1/2$ teaspoon grated orange zest
2 oranges, peeled, thinly sliced
1 small jicama, peeled, cut into julienne strips
16 strawberries, cut into halves

Place the Bibb lettuce, red leaf lettuce and onion in a salad bowl. Refrigerate, covered, until chilled.

Combine the oil, orange juice, vinegar, sugar, salad dressing mix and orange zest in a bowl. Toss the salad with a desired amount of the dressing. (Refrigerate the remaining dressing.) Add the oranges, jicama and strawberries to the top of the salad. *Yield: 8 servings.*

Crispy Romaine Salad

Sweet and Sour Dressing
1 cup vegetable oil
1 cup sugar
$^1/_2$ cup red wine vinegar
1 tablespoon soy sauce
Salt and pepper to taste

Salad
1 cup walnuts, chopped
1 (3-ounce) package ramen noodles, crumbled,
seasoning packet discarded
$^1/_4$ cup ($^1/_2$ stick) butter
1 bunch broccoli, separated into florets
1 head romaine, torn into pieces
4 green onions, chopped

For the sweet and sour dressing, combine the oil, sugar, vinegar, soy sauce, salt and pepper in a bowl. Chill, covered, until serving time.

For the salad, sauté the walnuts and noodles in the butter in a skillet until golden brown. Remove to paper towels; cool completely. Toss the broccoli, romaine, green onions, walnuts and noodles in a large bowl. When ready to serve, pour 1 cup of the dressing over the salad and toss. (Refrigerate the remaining dressing.) *Yield: 4 servings.*

B.L.T. Salad

12 slices bacon
2 cups (³/₄-inch) Italian bread cubes
Salt to taste
¹/₂ cup mayonnaise
2 tablespoons water
2 teaspoons fresh lemon juice
¹/₂ teaspoon minced garlic
Pepper to taste
2 heads Boston lettuce, torn into bite-size pieces
1 pound grape tomatoes, cut into halves
1 small red onion, sliced

Cook the bacon in a skillet until crisp. Remove to paper towels with a slotted spoon. Crumble and set aside. Pour off all but 2 tablespoons of the drippings. Heat the reserved drippings over medium heat until hot. Add the bread cubes and salt to taste. Sauté until golden brown, stirring constantly. Remove to paper towels to drain; cool.

Whisk the mayonnaise, water, lemon juice and garlic in a small bowl. Season with salt and pepper.

Toss the lettuce, tomatoes, onion, half the bacon and half the croutons in a large bowl with enough of the dressing to coat. Divide the salad among 4 plates. Top with the remaining bacon and croutons. *Yield: 4 servings*.

Spinach Salad

1 cup vegetable oil
¹/₂ cup sugar
¹/₃ cup ketchup
¹/₄ cup rice wine vinegar
1 medium onion, chopped
1 tablespoon Worcestershire sauce

1 bunch fresh spinach
2 hard-cooked eggs, sliced
¹/₂ cup sliced fresh mushrooms
1 (11-ounce) can mandarin oranges, drained
Croutons

Combine the oil, sugar, ketchup, vinegar, onion and Worcestershire sauce in a food processor and process until smooth. Refrigerate, covered, until chilled.

Combine the spinach, hard-cooked eggs, mushrooms, mandarin oranges and croutons in a large bowl. When ready to serve, pour a desired amount of the dressing over the salad and toss. (Refrigerate the remaining dressing.) *Yield: 4 servings.*

Strawberry Salad with Sesame Seed Dressing

¹/₂ cup vegetable oil
¹/₂ cup sugar
¹/₄ cup cider vinegar
2 tablespoons sesame seeds
1¹/₂ teaspoons poppy seeds
1¹/₂ teaspoons dried minced onion

¹/₄ teaspoon paprika
¹/₄ teaspoon Worcestershire sauce
1 pound green leaf lettuce, torn into pieces
¹/₂ cup sliced almonds
8 strawberries, sliced

Combine the oil, sugar, vinegar, sesame seeds, poppy seeds, onion, paprika and Worcestershire sauce in a bowl. Pour over the lettuce in a salad bowl. Top with the almonds and strawberries and toss. *Yield: 6 to 8 servings.*

Asian Slaw

2 (3-ounce) packages beef-flavor ramen noodles
2 (8-ounce) packages coleslaw mix
1 cup sliced almonds, toasted
1 bunch green onions, chopped
³/₄ cup vegetable oil
¹/₂ cup sugar
¹/₃ cup white vinegar

Remove the seasoning packets from the noodles; set aside. Crush the noodles and place in a large bowl. Top with the coleslaw mix, almonds and green onions.

Whisk the contents of the seasoning packets, oil, sugar and vinegar in a bowl. Pour over the slaw. Chill, covered, for 24 hours to blend the flavors. Toss the slaw before serving.
Yield: 8 to 10 servings.

Norwegian Slaw

3 heads cabbage, chopped or shredded
1 tablespoon salt
1 bunch celery, chopped
1 green bell pepper, chopped
4 cups sugar
2 cups vinegar
1 cup water
1 tablespoon celery seeds
1 tablespoon mustard seeds

Combine the cabbage and salt in a bowl. Let stand for 2 hours. Squeeze out the excess liquid. Add the celery and bell pepper; set aside.

Combine the sugar, vinegar, water, celery seeds and mustard seeds in a large saucepan. Bring to a boil. Boil for 5 minutes. Remove from the heat; cool completely. Pour over the cabbage mixture. Chill, covered, for 24 hours before serving. *Yield: 6 to 8 servings.*

NOTE: FOR ADDED COLOR, MAY USE BOTH RED AND GREEN CABBAGES. OTHER SHREDDED VEGETABLES, SUCH AS CARROTS AND BROCCOLI, MAY BE SUBSTITUTED FOR THE CELERY AND BELL PEPPER. POPPY SEEDS MAY ALSO BE ADDED.

Fresh Corn Salad

2 cups fresh corn kernels or frozen corn
kernels, thawed
1 yellow bell pepper, chopped
1 red bell pepper, chopped
1 red onion, minced

$^1/_2$ cup fresh cilantro, chopped
$^1/_4$ cup lime juice
$^1/_4$ cup olive oil
Salt and black pepper to taste

Combine the corn, bell peppers, onion, cilantro, lime juice, olive oil, salt and black pepper in a large bowl and toss. Refrigerate, covered, until chilled. *Yield: 8 servings.*

NOTE: MAY ALSO SERVE AS A DIP WITH CORN CHIPS.

Cucumber Salad

3 medium cucumbers, peeled, sliced
1$^1/_2$ cups finely chopped onions
1 green bell pepper, cut into strips
2 ribs celery, sliced
2 tablespoons chopped fresh parsley
$^1/_2$ cup vinegar

$^1/_4$ cup sugar
2 teaspoons salt
2 teaspoons lemon juice
1 teaspoon MSG
Black pepper to taste

Combine the cucumbers, onions, bell pepper, celery, parsley, vinegar, sugar, salt, lemon juice, MSG and black pepper in a bowl and mix well. Chill, covered, for 8 to 12 hours, stirring occasionally. *Yield: 6 servings.*

German Potato Salad

5 slices bacon
3/4 cup chopped onion
2 tablespoons flour
1 1/3 cups water
2/3 cup cider vinegar

1/4 cup sugar
1 teaspoon salt
1/8 teaspoon pepper
6 cups cooked sliced red or new potatoes

Cook the bacon in a large skillet until crisp. Remove to paper towels with a slotted spoon; crumble and set aside. Pour off all but 3 tablespoons of the drippings. Add the onion to the drippings. Cook until tender. Stir in the flour and mix well. Add the water and vinegar. Cook until bubbly and slightly thick, stirring constantly. Add the sugar, salt and pepper; stir until the sugar dissolves. Stir in the potatoes and bacon. Cook until heated through, stirring gently to coat the potato slices. Serve warm. *Yield: 6 to 8 servings.*

Marinated Vegetable Salad

2 cups broccoli florets, chopped
2 cups cauliflower florets, chopped
1 pint cherry tomatoes or grape tomatoes
1 small zucchini, chopped (3/4 cup)
3/4 cup chopped red bell pepper

3/4 cup chopped red onion
1/2 cup reduced-fat Italian salad dressing
1/2 cup balsamic vinegar
1/2 cup honey

Place the broccoli, cauliflower, tomatoes, zucchini, bell pepper and onion in a bowl. Combine the salad dressing, vinegar and honey in a bowl. Pour over the vegetables. Marinate, covered, in the refrigerator for at least 2 hours, stirring frequently to distribute the marinade evenly.
Yield: 6 to 8 servings.

Corn Bread Salad

1 cup sour cream
1 cup mayonnaise
1 (1-ounce) package ranch salad dressing mix
2 large tomatoes, chopped
$^1\!/_2$ cup chopped green onions
1 (9-inch) pan baked Mexican corn bread, crumbled
1 (16-ounce) can pinto beans, drained
1 cup (4 ounces) shredded Cheddar cheese
5 slices bacon, crisp-cooked, crumbled
1 (17-ounce) can whole kernel corn

Combine the sour cream, mayonnaise and salad dressing mix in a bowl. Combine the tomatoes and green onions in a bowl.

Layer the corn bread, beans, tomato mixture, cheese, bacon, corn and dressing $^1\!/_2$ at a time in a large bowl. Refrigerate, covered, until chilled. *Yield: 8 to 10 servings.*

Marinated cucumbers are a refreshing summer side salad and are so easy to make! Combine $^1\!/_4$ cup vinegar, 2 tablespoons sugar and $^1\!/_4$ teaspoon celery seeds in a bowl. Add 3 cups sliced cucumbers and toss to coat. Chill, covered, for at least 2 hours or up to 5 days.

67

Broccoli and Tortellini Salad

1 (7-ounce) package fresh
cheese tortellini
1 cup broccoli florets, blanched
$^1/_2$ cup finely chopped fresh parsley
$^1/_2$ cup Italian salad dressing
1 (6-ounce) jar marinated
artichoke hearts

$^1/_4$ cup sliced black olives
2 green onions, chopped
2 teaspoons chopped fresh basil
2 garlic cloves, minced
$^1/_2$ teaspoon oregano
5 or 6 cherry tomatoes, cut into halves
Grated Parmesan cheese to taste

Cook the tortellini according to the package directions; drain. Rinse under cold water; drain.
Combine the tortellini, broccoli, parsley, salad dressing, artichoke hearts, olives, green onions, basil, garlic and oregano in a large bowl. Chill, covered, for 6 to 12 hours to blend the flavors.
Just before serving, add the cherry tomatoes to the salad. Sprinkle with cheese.
Yield: 6 servings.

NOTE: IF PREPARING THIS SALAD A DAY IN ADVANCE, ADD THE BROCCOLI AND CHERRY TOMATOES JUST BEFORE SERVING.

Fruit and Cheese Tortellini

1 (7-ounce) package frozen cheese
tortellini
1 cup halved grapes

1 cup blueberries
1 cup strawberries, sliced
Poppy seed salad dressing to taste

Cook the tortellini according to the package directions; drain and cool. Combine the tortellini, grapes, blueberries, strawberries and salad dressing in a bowl. Serve immediately. *Yield: 8 servings.*

Cranberry Salad

2 (3-ounce) packages cherry gelatin
1 cup miniature marshmallows (optional)
½ cup sugar
2 cups boiling water
1 cup orange juice

1 pound fresh cranberries, finely chopped
2 large apples, finely chopped
1 (8-ounce) can crushed pineapple, drained
½ cup chopped pecans

Dissolve the gelatin, marshmallows and sugar in the boiling water in a large heatproof serving bowl. Cool for 10 minutes.

Add the orange juice, cranberries, apples, pineapple and pecans and mix well. Chill until firm. *Yield: 8 servings.*

NOTE: MAY CHOP THE CRANBERRIES AND APPLES IN A FOOD PROCESSOR.

Champagne Salad

8 ounces cream cheese, softened
¾ cup sugar
12 ounces frozen strawberries, thawed
1 (20-ounce) can crushed pineapple, drained

2 bananas, coarsely chopped
1 cup chopped pecans
1 (8-ounce) container whipped topping, thawed

Combine the cream cheese and sugar in a bowl. Add the strawberries, pineapple, bananas, pecans and whipped topping. Freeze for 30 minutes before serving. *Yield: 10 servings.*

Maxine's Beef, Blue Cheese and Walnut Salad

Maxine's Cafe and Bakery

70

Marinade

$^1/_2$ cup vegetable oil	2 garlic cloves, coarsely chopped
$^1/_2$ cup red wine vinegar	
2 tablespoons brown sugar	$2^1/_2$ to 3 pounds flank steak or beef tenderloin

Vinaigrette

$1^1/_2$ cups vegetable oil	$1^1/_2$ teaspoons chopped fresh rosemary
$^1/_2$ cup red wine vinegar	
2 tablespoons sugar	$^3/_4$ teaspoon salt
$1^1/_2$ teaspoons fresh thyme leaves	$^1/_2$ teaspoon pepper

Salad

Watercress	1 cup walnuts
Curly endive	6 to 8 ounces blue cheese, crumbled
Roma tomatoes, cut into quarters	

For *the marinade*, combine the oil, vinegar, brown sugar and garlic in a large sealable plastic bag. Add the flank steak and seal the bag. Marinate in the refrigerator for 8 to 12 hours. Remove the steak from the marinade; discard the marinade. Broil or grill the steak (or roast or grill the tenderloin) until done to taste. Let stand for 10 minutes. Slice or julienne the steak; set aside.

For *the vinaigrette*, combine the oil, vinegar, sugar, thyme, rosemary, salt and pepper in a bowl and mix well. Toss the steak with enough of the vinaigrette to coat.

For *the salad*, arrange the steak on a bed of watercress and endive. Top with the tomatoes. Sprinkle with the walnuts and cheese.
Yield: *8 servings.*

NOTE: MAY SUBSTITUTE ANY LETTUCE EXCEPT ICEBERG FOR THE CURLY ENDIVE.

Chicken Caesar Salad

Maxine's Cafe and Bakery

¹/₄ cup red wine vinegar
¹/₄ cup lemon juice
¹/₃ cup grated Parmesan cheese
2 tablespoons Dijon mustard
1 tablespoon coarsely ground black pepper
2 teaspoons anchovy paste
1¹/₂ cups vegetable oil
3 cups chopped cooked chicken breast
1¹/₂ cups herbed croutons
¹/₂ cup chopped red bell pepper
¹/₄ to ¹/₂ cup slivered red onion
¹/₄ cup toasted pine nuts

Combine the vinegar, lemon juice, cheese, Dijon mustard, black pepper and anchovy paste in a food processor or blender and process until smooth. Add the oil gradually, processing constantly until smooth; set aside.

Toss the chicken, croutons, bell pepper, onion and pine nuts together in a salad bowl. Add enough of the dressing to coat and toss again. Serve immediately. *Yield: 6 servings.*

NOTE: ANCHOVY PASTE IS AVAILABLE AT ITALIAN MARKETS OR GOURMET FOOD STORES.

More tips from Maxine's Café and Bakery...

When baking, line cookie sheets and brownie pans with foil, then lightly coat the foil with nonstick cooking spray. This saves time when cleaning up and helps to keep the food from sticking to the pan. With bar cookies, such as brownies or lemon bars, either refrigerate or freeze the cookies in the pan. Once cold or frozen, just lift the bars out of the pan with the foil, peel off the foil, and cut to the desired size.

71

Cherry Almond Chicken Salad

1 (12-ounce) can chicken breast meat, drained
3/4 cup mayonnaise
1/2 cup dried cherries
1/4 cup slivered almonds, toasted
1/2 cup chopped celery
1/4 teaspoon onion salt

Combine the chicken, mayonnaise, dried cherries, almonds, celery and onion salt in a medium bowl and mix well. Chill, covered, for 1 hour. Yield: 3 *servings*.

NOTE: THIS SALAD DOES NOT HAVE TO BE CHILLED BEFORE SERVING, BUT IT TASTES BEST CHILLED.

Fruited Chicken Salad

2 (6-ounce) packages mixed long grain and wild rice
2 or 3 chicken breasts, cooked, chopped
1 1/2 cups cashews
1 (11-ounce) can mandarin oranges, drained
1 (8-ounce) can pineapple tidbits, drained
1 (8-ounce) can sliced water chestnuts, drained
8 ounces seedless green grapes
2/3 cup mayonnaise
1/2 cup milk
1/2 small onion, chopped
Juice of 1 lemon

Cook the rice according to the package directions. Combine the rice, chicken, cashews, mandarin oranges, pineapple, water chestnuts, grapes, mayonnaise, milk, onion and lemon juice in a bowl and mix well. Serve warm or chilled. Yield: 10 *servings*.

Oriental Chicken Salad

1 (7-ounce) package maifun
Vegetable oil for frying
1 head lettuce, shredded
6 chicken breasts, cooked, shredded
2 bunches scallions, chopped
3/4 cup vegetable oil
9 tablespoons rice vinegar
6 tablespoons sugar
1 1/2 teaspoons dry mustard
4 1/2 ounces slivered almonds

Fry 1/4 of the maifun at a time in 3 inches hot oil in a skillet according to the package directions; drain on paper towels. Combine half the maifun with the lettuce, chicken and scallions in a large bowl; set aside.

Combine 3/4 cup oil, the vinegar, sugar and dry mustard in a bowl. Pour over the salad and toss to mix. Arrange the remaining maifun on a serving platter. Spoon the salad over the maifun. Top with the almonds and additional scallions if desired. *Yield: 8 servings.*

NOTE: MAIFUN ARE ASIAN RICE NOODLES AND ARE AVAILABLE AT ASIAN MARKETS OR GOURMET FOOD STORES.

Southwest Grilled Chicken Salad

3 tablespoons salsa
2 tablespoons ranch salad dressing
3 ounces boneless chicken, grilled, cut into bite-size pieces
2 cups chopped lettuce
1 small tomato, chopped (about $1/2$ cup)
$1/4$ cup corn kernels, cooked
2 tablespoons shredded Cheddar cheese
1 tablespoon chopped fresh cilantro
5 or 6 tortilla chips, crushed (about $1/3$ cup)

Combine the salsa and salad dressing in a bowl; set aside. Combine the chicken, lettuce, tomato, corn, cheese, cilantro and tortilla chips in a bowl. Top with the salsa dressing and serve. *Yield: 1 serving.*

NOTE: MAY USE PRECOOKED GRILLED CHICKEN BREAST STRIPS. MAY ADD A DESIRED AMOUNT OF DRAINED CANNED BLACK BEANS. FAT-FREE RANCH DRESSING MAY BE SUBSTITUTED FOR THE REGULAR RANCH DRESSING.

Main Street used to be very popular, and you could easily take the city bus downtown for lunch. Hermann's on Main Street was a favorite lunch spot and specialized in sodas, sundaes, and desserts. People would line up on Main Street waiting to buy a ticket to see the latest movie . . . the hotels would host dances. Downtown Evansville was **the** *hot spot until the suburbs began to develop.*

Billie Dees

Chilled Shrimp and Linguini Salad

Dressing

³/₄ cup olive oil
¹/₃ cup red wine vinegar
2 tablespoons chopped fresh basil
2 tablespoons chopped fresh rosemary

1 teaspoon oregano (optional)
1 teaspoon parsley (optional)
1 garlic clove, minced
Salt and pepper to taste

Salad

16 ounces linguini
8 ounces deveined peeled medium
  shrimp, cooked
1 red bell pepper, chopped
1 yellow bell pepper, chopped

6 green onions, chopped
¹/₄ cup sliced sun-dried tomatoes
1 (3-ounce) jar capers, drained (optional)
1 (2-ounce) can sliced black olives,
  drained

For the dressing, combine the olive oil, vinegar, basil, rosemary, oregano, parsley, garlic, salt and pepper in a bowl; set aside.

For the salad, cook the linguini according to the package directions; drain. Rinse under cold water; drain. Combine the pasta, shrimp, bell peppers, green onions, sun-dried tomatoes, capers and olives in a bowl. Pour the dressing over the salad and mix well. Chill, covered, for at least 2 hours before serving. Yield: 10 servings.

NOTE: MAY BE PREPARED UP TO 12 HOURS IN ADVANCE.

Fresh Lemon, Tuna and White Bean Salad

To zest a lemon, gently grate the yellow part of the lemon peel using a citrus zester or the smallest holes on a grater. Don't grate the white pith since it tastes bitter. After removing the zest, squeeze the juice from the lemon.

$1/4$ cup fresh lemon juice
2 tablespoons olive oil
1 teaspoon grated lemon zest
$1/2$ teaspoon salt
$1/2$ teaspoon pepper
1 cup chopped peeled cucumber
$1/4$ cup minced red onion
2 tablespoons capers
1 tablespoon chopped parsley
1 (15-ounce) can cannellini beans, rinsed, drained
1 (12-ounce) can solid white albacore tuna, drained

Whisk the lemon juice, olive oil, lemon zest, salt and pepper in a large bowl. Stir in the cucumber, onion, capers and parsley. Fold in the beans and tuna. Serve immediately or chill. Serve with crackers, over salad greens or inside hollowed-out tomatoes. *Yield: 4 servings.*

NOTE: FOR A COLD SALAD, CHILL THE BEANS AND TUNA BEFORE PREPARING THE SALAD.

Smoked Sausage and Feta Cheese Pasta Salad

$^1/_4$ cup balsamic vinegar
3 tablespoons water
1 envelope Italian salad dressing mix
$^1/_4$ cup water
$^1/_4$ cup olive oil
8 ounces tricolor rotini
7 ounces low-fat smoked sausage
4 ounces feta cheese, crumbled
1 stalk broccoli, chopped ($1^1/_4$ cups)
2 small tomatoes, chopped ($^3/_4$ cup)
$^1/_2$ green bell pepper, chopped ($^1/_2$ cup)
$^1/_2$ cup chopped red onion

Combine the vinegar, 3 tablespoons water and salad dressing mix in a bowl or cruet. Stir or shake vigorously until well blended. Add $^1/_4$ cup water and the olive oil and stir or shake again until well blended; set aside.

Cook the rotini according to the package directions; drain. Cut the sausage lengthwise and crosswise into quarters. Slice each quarter into bite-size pieces. Combine the pasta, sausage, cheese, broccoli, tomatoes, bell pepper, onion and dressing in a large bowl. Chill, covered, for 1 hour. *Yield: 8 servings.*

NOTE: MAY SUBSTITUTE **1** CUP BOTTLED BALSAMIC VINAIGRETTE FOR THE DRESSING. MAY SUBSTITUTE ANY VEGETABLES YOU HAVE ON HAND FOR THOSE LISTED. RECIPE MAY BE DOUBLED.

77

The Plot Thickens

A Haunted Library

It was a dark and stormy night…in the winter of 1937, as the janitor at Evansville's Willard Library went about his duties. Alone in the dark and bitter cold, he made his way to the basement, where he planned to shovel coal into the furnace. He scanned the room with a flashlight in hand, cautious of any nighttime visitors. He was not expecting, however, to come face to face with a ghostly veiled lady dressed from head to toe in glowing grey! The janitor stood motionless, paralyzed with fear. Yet as suddenly as she appeared, the specter disappeared, leaving the frightened and confused janitor alone in the darkness.

Since that fateful evening, there have been numerous sightings and strange happenings at the Willard Library, often involving the infamous "Grey Lady," who has appeared to library staff as a shadowy grey female apparition. Bathroom faucets have been mysteriously turned on (once while a librarian was actually in the room!) while others have reported feeling an eerie draft of cold air. These unexplained events have often been accompanied by the strong, cloying scent of heavy perfume.

Who is this "Lady in Grey"? The glowing apparition is believed to be the ghost of Louise Carpenter, the daughter of library founder Willard Carpenter. She believed her father was of "unsound mind" when he established the library and, after an acrimonious lawsuit, lost claim to any of the library's property. The legend claims that after her death, she returned to Willard Library and will haunt the library until the property is returned to the surviving heirs of the Willard Carpenter family.

Today, people from all over the world watch and wait for shadowy figures to appear on Willard Library's "ghostcam," which can be found at www.Libraryghost.com.

Disgruntled ghosts aside, there's more to be found among the stacks at Willard. The state's oldest public library boasts an impressive collection of genealogical resources and historic photographs. As you're browsing, just remember what happened…*once upon a time*!

Soups

Tuscan White Bean Soup

Victoria National Golf Club, Chef Douglas Rennie, C.E.C.

2¹/₂ cups dried Great Northern beans (about 15 ounces),
sorted, soaked 8 to 12 hours
2 quarts cold water
1 sprig of fresh rosemary
2 fresh sage leaves
2 bay leaves
1 tablespoon extra-virgin olive oil
1 medium yellow onion, coarsely chopped
(about 1¹/₂ cups)
¹/₂ teaspoon each basil and salt
Pepper to taste
6 garlic cloves, finely chopped
¹/₄ cup white wine
1 (8-ounce) can tomatoes, chopped
¹/₂ teaspoon salt
Salt to taste

Drain and rinse the beans. Place them in a soup pot. Add the water, rosemary, sage and bay leaves. Bring to a boil. Reduce the heat to low. Simmer for 30 to 35 minutes or until the beans are very soft and beginning to break apart. Remove and discard the herbs. Reserve 1 cup of the beans. Remove the remaining beans with a slotted spoon to a food processor. Process until smooth, adding the bean cooking liquid or water as needed. Return the puréed beans to the pot. Cook over low heat.

Heat the olive oil in a sauté pan. Add the onion, basil, ¹/₂ teaspoon salt and a few pinches of pepper. Sauté over medium heat for about 7 minutes or until the onion is tender. Add the garlic. Sauté for about 2 minutes. Stir in the wine. Cook for 1 to 2 minutes or until almost all the liquid has evaporated from the pan. Add the tomatoes. Simmer for 10 minutes.

Stir the tomato mixture, reserved beans, ¹/₂ teaspoon salt and a few pinches of pepper into the puréed beans. Cook, covered, over low heat for 30 minutes. Thin the soup with a little water if necessary and season with salt and pepper. Serve with Corn Bread with Smoked Cheese and Chiles (page 82). *Yield: 6 to 8 servings.*

Corn Bread with Smoked Cheese and Chiles

Victoria National Golf Club, Chef Douglas Rennie, C.E.C.

1 tablespoon unsalted butter
Kernels from 1 ear of corn (about ³⁄₄ cup)
Pinch of salt
Pinch of cayenne pepper
1¹⁄₄ cups milk
¹⁄₂ cup (1 stick) unsalted butter
1¹⁄₂ cups flour
1 cup fine cornmeal
2 tablespoons sugar
1 tablespoon baking powder
2 eggs, beaten
1 ounce shredded smoked Gouda cheese (about ¹⁄₂ cup)
1 jalapeño or serrano chile, seeded, chopped

Melt 1 tablespoon butter in a small sauté pan. Add the corn, salt and cayenne pepper. Sauté for about 5 minutes or until the corn is tender. Remove from the heat; set aside.

Heat the milk and ¹⁄₂ cup butter in a saucepan over medium heat until the butter is melted. Remove from the heat. Combine the flour, cornmeal, sugar and baking powder in a bowl and mix well. Whisk the eggs into the warm milk mixture. Pour the egg mixture into the dry ingredients. Add the corn, cheese and jalapeño chile. Stir just until combined. Do not overmix.

Spread the batter in a greased 9-inch round baking pan. Bake at 375 degrees for 20 to 25 minutes or until the top springs back when lightly touched or a wooden pick inserted into the center comes out clean. *Yield: 12 servings.*

Vegetarian Black Bean Soup

1 (14-ounce) can vegetable broth, divided
1 cup chopped onion
2 garlic cloves, minced
2 (15-ounce) cans black beans, rinsed, drained
1 cup coarsely chopped peeled potatoes
$\frac{1}{2}$ teaspoon thyme
$\frac{1}{2}$ teaspoon cumin
1 (14-ounce) can diced tomatoes
$\frac{1}{4}$ to $\frac{1}{2}$ teaspoon hot red pepper sauce
2 green onions, sliced

Combine $\frac{1}{4}$ cup of the broth, the chopped onion and garlic in a saucepan. Bring to a boil. Reduce the heat to low. Simmer, covered, for 6 to 8 minutes or until the onion is tender. Stir in the beans, potatoes, thyme, cumin and remaining broth. Return to a boil. Reduce the heat to low. Simmer, covered, for 20 to 25 minutes or until the potatoes are tender. Stir in the tomatoes and pepper sauce. Cook until heated through. Sprinkle with the green onions. *Yield: 6 servings*.

White Bean and Chicken Soup

3 tablespoons olive oil
1 large white onion, chopped
3 garlic cloves, minced
1 pound boneless skinless chicken breasts, cut into thin strips
1 tablespoon cumin
1 teaspoon oregano
4 cups chicken broth
2 (15-ounce) cans cannellini beans, rinsed, drained
1 cup water
2 (4-ounce) cans diced green chiles
Salt and pepper to taste
$\frac{1}{4}$ cup fresh cilantro leaves, chopped

Heat the olive oil in a Dutch oven over high heat. Add the onion and garlic. Cook for 2 to 3 minutes, stirring constantly to prevent the garlic from burning. Add the chicken, cumin and oregano and stir to coat the ingredients with the seasonings. Cook for about 5 minutes or until the chicken begins to brown, stirring frequently. Add 2 cups of the chicken broth to the pan, stirring to deglaze. Add the remaining 2 cups chicken broth, beans, water and green chiles. Simmer, covered, for 45 minutes. (May simmer longer at a lower heat, if necessary.) Season with salt and pepper.

Ladle the soup into bowls. Sprinkle with the cilantro. Garnish with dollops of sour cream if desired. Serve with your favorite corn bread. *Yield: 4 to 6 servings.*

Lima Bean Soup

3 (14-ounce) cans chicken broth
2 (15-ounce) cans lima beans, rinsed, drained
3 medium carrots, thinly sliced
2 medium potatoes, peeled, coarsely chopped
2 small red bell peppers, chopped
2 small onions, chopped
2 ribs celery, thinly sliced
$^1/_4$ cup ($^1/_2$ stick) butter or margarine
1$^1/_2$ teaspoons marjoram
$^1/_2$ teaspoon oregano
$^1/_2$ teaspoon salt
$^1/_2$ teaspoon black pepper
1 cup half-and-half
3 slices bacon, crisp-cooked, crumbled

Combine the chicken broth, lima beans, carrots, potatoes, bell peppers, onions, celery, butter, marjoram, oregano, salt and black pepper in a soup pot. Bring to a boil over medium heat. Reduce the heat to low. Simmer, covered, for 25 to 35 minutes or until the vegetables are tender. Add the half-and-half. Cook until heated through but do not boil. Let the soup cool slightly. Purée the soup in batches in a blender or food processor. Return the soup to the pot and heat through. Sprinkle with the bacon just before serving. Yield: 10 to 12 servings.

Caramelized Onion and Mushroom Soup

1 tablespoon butter
1 $\frac{1}{2}$ pounds onions, halved, thinly sliced
4 sprigs of fresh thyme
2 tablespoons butter
1 $\frac{1}{2}$ pounds portobello mushrooms, stemmed, halved and
cut into $\frac{1}{4}$-inch strips
3 tablespoons brandy
3 garlic cloves, minced
8 cups beef broth
1 cup dry white wine
Salt and pepper to taste

Melt 1 tablespoon butter in a large heavy pot over high heat. Add the onions and thyme. Sauté for 8 minutes or until the onions begin to soften. Reduce the heat to low. Cook for 20 minutes or until the onions are caramelized, stirring occasionally. Remove to a medium bowl; set aside.

Melt 2 tablespoons butter in the same pot over medium-high heat. Add the mushrooms. Sauté for about 12 minutes or until tender. Add the brandy and garlic. Stir for 20 seconds. Stir in the caramelized onion mixture, beef broth and wine. Bring to a boil. Reduce the heat to low. Simmer for about 45 minutes or until the onions are very tender. Remove and discard the thyme. Season with salt and pepper. Serve warm. *Yield: 6 servings.*

NOTE: FOR A HEARTY MAIN-DISH SOUP, STIR IN LEFTOVER STEAK.

French Onion Soup

5 cups thinly sliced onions
2 tablespoons butter
2 tablespoons olive oil
$1/2$ teaspoon salt
$1/4$ teaspoon sugar
3 tablespoons flour
8 cups beef broth, warmed
$1/2$ cup dry white wine
1 large tomato, chopped
8 slices French bread, buttered
Shredded Swiss cheese to taste

Sauté the onions in the butter and olive oil in a large pot until tender. Reduce the heat to low. Cook, covered, for 25 minutes. Stir in the salt and sugar. Cook, uncovered, over medium heat for 40 minutes or until light brown, stirring frequently. Remove from the heat. Stir in the flour. Return to the heat. Add the beef broth. Bring to a boil. Stir in the wine and tomato. Simmer for 30 to 40 minutes.

Ladle the soup into 8 ovenproof bowls. Top each with a bread slice. Sprinkle cheese over the bread. Broil until the cheese melts and the bread is toasted. *Yield: 8 servings.*

I was a sophomore and my friend was a senior at the University of Evansville. One day, he was walking across the front lawn from the Union Building, and I decided to sneak up and surprise him. I ran up from behind and attempted to jump onto his back. Unfortunately, he ducked to the ground at the exact moment I leapt off the ground. I landed chin-first onto the concrete! He brought me back to his apartment to get cleaned up and assured me I looked fine. This was the moment I saw my friend in a different light. This friend is now my husband!

Karyn Staples

87

Baked Potato Soup

4 large baking potatoes
$^2/_3$ cup butter or margarine
$^2/_3$ cup flour
5 to 6 cups milk
1$^1/_4$ cups (5 ounces) shredded Cheddar cheese
12 slices bacon, crisp-cooked, crumbled
4 green onions, chopped
$^3/_4$ teaspoon salt
$^1/_4$ teaspoon pepper
8 ounces sour cream

Scrub the potatoes and prick in several places with a fork. Bake at 400 degrees for 1 hour or until tender. Cool completely. Cut the potatoes lengthwise into halves. Scoop out the pulp; set aside. Discard the skins.

Melt the butter in a heavy saucepan over low heat. Add the flour and stir until smooth. Cook for 1 minute, stirring constantly. Add 5 cups milk gradually. Cook over medium heat until thickened and bubbly, stirring constantly. Stir in the potato pulp, 1 cup of the cheese, $^1/_2$ cup of the bacon, 2 tablespoons of the green onions, the salt and pepper. Cook over low heat until heated through. Stir in the sour cream and additional milk, if necessary, to achieve the desired consistency. Serve garnished with the remaining cheese, bacon and green onions.
Yield: 6 to 8 servings.

Spinach, Sausage and Pasta Soup

1 pound sweet Italian sausage, casings removed
2 medium onions, chopped
4 garlic cloves, minced
2 (15-ounce) cans Great Northern beans
1 (28-ounce) can plum tomatoes
2 (14-ounce) cans chicken broth
5 ounces fresh spinach, stems removed, chopped
6 ounces (1 cup) tubetti pasta, cooked, drained
Grated Parmesan cheese (optional)

Brown the sausage in a saucepan, stirring until crumbly. Add the onions and garlic. Sauté for 2 minutes. Add the beans, tomatoes, chicken broth, spinach and pasta. Simmer for 10 minutes or until heated through. Serve with cheese if desired. *Yield: 6 servings.*

NOTE: THIS SOUP TASTES EVEN BETTER WHEN THE FLAVORS ARE ALLOWED TO BLEND IN THE REFRIGERATOR FOR 8 TO 12 HOURS.

You're so "Evansville" if you know the difference between a corn dog and a pronto pup! A corn dog is a hot dog on a stick fried in a cornmeal batter. A pronto pup is a hot dog on a stick fried with pancake batter. You can get corn dogs and pronto pups at community festivals and county fairs. Since I am a pancake lover, I prefer the pronto pups. They are so good!

Ellen Spence

Butternut Squash Bisque

1 tablespoon vegetable oil
3 medium leeks, white parts only, coarsely chopped
(about 1 cup)
2 large garlic cloves, minced
1 large butternut squash, peeled, seeded and cut into 2-inch chunks
(about 7 cups)
4 to 4^1/$_2$ cups chicken stock or low-sodium chicken broth
^{1}/$_2$ teaspoon salt
^{1}/$_2$ teaspoon nutmeg
^{1}/$_2$ teaspoon cumin
Freshly ground pepper to taste
1^1/$_4$ cups canned corn kernels or thawed frozen corn kernels
3 tablespoons heavy cream

Heat the oil in a large saucepan over medium-high heat. Add the leeks and garlic. Cook until tender, stirring frequently. Add the squash, 4 cups chicken stock, salt, nutmeg, cumin and pepper. Bring to a boil. Reduce the heat to low. Simmer, covered, for about 25 minutes or until the squash is very soft.

Strain the vegetables, reserving the cooking liquid. Purée the vegetables in batches in a blender or food processor until smooth, adding the reserved cooking liquid as needed to achieve the desired consistency. Return the vegetable purée to the saucepan with the reserved cooking liquid. Stir in the corn, cream and additional chicken stock, if needed, to achieve a medium-thick consistency. Taste and adjust the seasonings. Cook until heated through. Serve hot, garnished with fresh chopped chives, heavy cream and molasses. *Yield: 10 to 12 servings.*

Zucchini Soup

2 pounds ground sirloin
2 large ribs celery, chopped
1 onion, chopped
2 zucchini, sliced
2 (28-ounce) cans diced tomatoes
1 (26-ounce) jar pasta sauce
1 tablespoon Italian seasoning
1 tablespoon oregano
1 teaspoon chopped fresh basil
1 teaspoon minced garlic
1 green bell pepper, chopped
1 red bell pepper, chopped
Shredded mozzarella cheese to taste
Freshly grated Parmesan cheese to taste

Brown the ground sirloin in a saucepan, stirring until crumbly; drain. Add the celery and onion. Cook for about 10 minutes, stirring constantly. Stir in the zucchini, tomatoes, pasta sauce, Italian seasoning, oregano, basil and garlic. Simmer, covered, for 20 minutes. Add the bell peppers. Simmer, covered, for 10 minutes. Ladle the soup into bowls. Sprinkle with mozzarella and Parmesan cheese.
Yield: 6 to 8 servings.

Evansville's annual Fall Festival is known for featuring unusual things to eat. Some unique offerings have included: fried candy bars; fried Twinkies; fried pickles; alligator jerky; kangaroo jerky; chocolate-covered crickets; squid on a stick; snail poppers; and gator gumbo. And finally . . . fried brain sandwiches!

91

Spicy Cheeseburger Soup

2 cups cubed peeled potatoes
1$^1/_2$ cups water
2 small carrots, shredded
1 small onion, chopped
$^1/_4$ cup chopped green bell pepper
1 jalapeño chile, seeded, chopped
1 garlic clove, minced
1 tablespoon beef bouillon granules
$^1/_2$ teaspoon salt
1 pound ground beef, browned, drained
2$^1/_2$ cups milk
3 tablespoons flour
8 ounces Velveeta cheese, cut into cubes
$^1/_2$ teaspoon cayenne pepper
8 ounces bacon slices, crisp-cooked, crumbled

Combine the potatoes, water, carrots, onion, bell pepper, jalapeño chile, garlic, bouillon and salt in a saucepan. Bring to a boil. Reduce the heat to low. Simmer, covered, for 15 minutes or until the potatoes are tender. Stir in the ground beef and 2 cups of the milk. Cook until heated through.

Combine the remaining $^1/_2$ cup milk and flour in a bowl. Stir into the soup gradually. Return to a boil. Cook for 2 minutes or until thick and bubbly. Reduce the heat to low. Add the Velveeta cheese and stir until melted. Stir in the cayenne pepper. Top with the bacon just before serving. *Yield: 6 to 8 servings.*

Burgoo

The Old Mill Restaurant

3 pounds potatoes, peeled
6 medium onions
1 small head cabbage
3 carrots
$^1/_2$ bunch celery
3 cups fresh lima beans or thawed frozen lima beans
3 cups fresh green beans or thawed frozen green beans
3 cups cooked navy beans
2 cups fresh corn kernels or thawed frozen corn kernels
2 cups fresh peas or thawed frozen peas
1 (3-pound) beef roast, cooked, ground (include broth)
$^1/_2$ small chicken, cooked, ground (include broth)
1 quart tomato juice
Salt and pepper to taste

Coarsely chop the potatoes, onions, cabbage, carrots, celery, beans, corn and peas in batches in a food processor fitted with a steel blade. Combine the chopped vegetables, beef, chicken, beef broth, chicken broth and tomato juice in a large heavy pot. Add enough water to cover the ingredients. Bring to a boil. Reduce the heat to low. Simmer for 2 to 3 hours, stirring frequently and adding water as needed to prevent sticking and scorching. Season with salt and pepper during the last 30 minutes of cooking. *Yield: 24 servings.*

Evansville's annual Freedom Festival lights up the Ohio River for one week at the end of each June into July. Special events on the Riverfront include Thunder on the Ohio unlimited hydroplane races, Thunder Air Show, and a spectacular fireworks display accompanied by the sounds of the Evansville Philharmonic Orchestra and the Evansville Symphonic Band. Thousands of visitors come down to the river to enjoy these festivities, which also include hot air balloons, food booths, carnival rides, and a parade.

Habanero Chili

2 pounds ground sirloin
1 large onion, puréed in a food processor
4 (15-ounce) cans hot chili beans
1 (15-ounce) can tomato sauce
1 garlic clove, chopped
$^1/_4$ teaspoon ground habanero pepper
Salt to taste

Brown the ground sirloin in a saucepan, stirring until crumbly; drain. Add the onion, beans, tomato sauce, garlic, habanero pepper and salt. Simmer for 4 hours. Serve over pasta topped with shredded Colby Jack cheese if desired. *Yield: 8 servings.*

NOTE: THIS CHILI TASTES EVEN BETTER THE DAY AFTER IT'S MADE.

Hearty Turkey Chili

1 pound ground turkey breast
2 tablespoons canola oil
2 tablespoons hot chili oil
1½ cups coarsely chopped white onions
1 (15-ounce) can tomato sauce
1 (14-ounce) can tomatoes
1 (6-ounce) can tomato paste
1 cup water
1 envelope chili seasoning mix
1 (15-ounce) can black beans
1½ cups coarsely chopped green bell peppers
1½ cups coarsely chopped mushrooms
1 cup coarsely chopped celery
Salt and freshly ground black pepper to taste
¾ cup chopped fresh parsley

Cook the turkey in the canola oil and chili oil in a Dutch oven over medium heat for 3 to 5 minutes or until crumbly and cooked through. Add additional oil to the pan if needed. Add the onions. Cook for 3 to 5 minutes. Stir in the tomato sauce, undrained tomatoes, tomato paste, water and chili seasoning mix and mix well. Add the beans, bell peppers, mushrooms and celery. Bring to a simmer. Simmer, covered, for 1 hour. Season with salt and black pepper. Stir in the parsley or sprinkle over each serving. Garnish each serving with sour cream, crushed red pepper, hot red pepper sauce and jalapeño chiles as desired. Serve with your favorite corn bread. *Yield: 8 servings.*

Two Sides to
Every Story

The Fall Festival—
A West Side Story

Every year, Evansville hosts an amazing street festival that transforms the city's West Side for one week in October. Rumored to be the second largest street festival in the United States (drawing up to 60,000 visitors per day!), the West Side Nut Club Fall Festival offers a vast selection of unique foods, carnival rides, parades, and nightly entertainment.

With 122 food booths competing for space on both sides of historic West Franklin Street, almost any kind of dietary delight (or disaster!) may be found. Local booster clubs, churches, and other charitable organizations operate food booths featuring their "signature" treats. Unusual foods are a Fall Festival tradition—nothing, it seems, is too strange to be dipped in batter or covered in chocolate. Adventurous types can sample snail poppers, breaded pickle spears, corn nuggets, chocolate-covered crickets, deep-fried candy bars, gator gumbo, and the ever-popular brain sandwich. Not to worry! Dozen of booths serve more conventional street festival fare such as corn dogs, hamburgers, bratwurst, and lemon shake-ups. If it can be fried, it's certain to be found here—over 2,500 gallons of grease are collected from the food booths during the week! Festival-goers are often seen plotting their search for their favorite festival food on the widely distributed "munchie maps."

But the Fall Festival is much more than just a celebration of food and fun—it is a way to strengthen our community. The festival was created in 1921 by the West Side Nut Club, a philanthropic organization that has distributed over $1,600,000 to various local causes. The Nut Club's motto is "From Small Acorns, Large Oaks Grow." This motto reflects the Club's long-standing commitment to Evansville's children. For many reasons, the Fall Festival is a beloved Evansville tradition that, like an oak tree, has grown to great heights. All this, from just a seed of an idea that was planted…*once upon a time.*

Vegetables and Side Dishes

Apple Cranberry Bake

3 cups chopped peeled apples
2 tablespoons fresh cranberries
2 tablespoons flour
1 cup sugar
3 envelopes cinnamon-spice
instant oatmeal

³/₄ cup chopped pecans
¹/₂ cup flour
¹/₂ cup packed brown sugar
¹/₂ cup (1 stick) butter, melted

Combine the apples, cranberries and 2 tablespoons flour in a bowl, tossing to coat the fruit. Add the sugar and mix well. Spoon into a lightly greased 2-quart or 9×13-inch baking dish.

Combine the uncooked oatmeal, pecans, ¹/₂ cup flour and brown sugar in a bowl. Add the butter and mix well. Sprinkle over the fruit. Bake at 350 degrees for 45 minutes. *Yield: 6 to 8 servings.*

Holiday Cranberries

2 cups fresh cranberries
¹/₂ cup sugar
¹/₂ cup chopped pecans
2 eggs

1 cup sugar
1 cup flour
¹/₂ cup (1 stick) butter, melted
¹/₄ cup shortening, melted

Place the cranberries in a greased 10-inch pie plate. Sprinkle with ¹/₂ cup sugar and the pecans; set aside.

Beat the eggs in a bowl. Beat in 1 cup sugar gradually. Add the flour, butter and shortening and mix well. Pour over the cranberries. Bake at 325 degrees for 1 hour. *Yield: 6 to 8 servings.*

Artichoke Florentine

1 (14-ounce) can quartered artichoke
  hearts, drained
2 (6-ounce) jars marinated artichoke
  hearts, drained
12 ounces cream cheese, softened
1 (10-ounce) package frozen chopped
  spinach, thawed, squeezed dry

1 cup (4 ounces) freshly grated Parmesan
  cheese
1/2 cup mayonnaise
3 garlic cloves, pressed
1 tablespoon lemon juice
12 sheets frozen phyllo dough, thawed

Combine the artichoke hearts, cream cheese, spinach, cheese, mayonnaise, garlic and lemon juice in a bowl. Layer the phyllo sheets and artichoke mixture alternately in a greased 9×9-inch baking pan until all the ingredients are used, ending with a phyllo sheet. Bake at 375 degrees for 30 minutes. Serve as a side dish or as an appetizer with chips or crackers. *Yield: 8 to 10 servings.*

Simple Roasted Asparagus

1 pound fresh asparagus
3 tablespoons olive oil
1/2 teaspoon sugar

1/4 teaspoon salt
1/4 teaspoon freshly ground pepper

Snap off and discard the tough ends of the asparagus spears. Arrange in a single layer on a baking sheet. Drizzle with the olive oil. Broil about 5 inches from the heat source for 4 minutes. Sprinkle with the sugar, salt and pepper. *Yield: 4 servings.*

Asparagus Vinaigrette

$^1/_4$ cup tarragon vinegar
2 teaspoons Dijon mustard
$1^1/_2$ teaspoons fresh lemon juice
$1^1/_2$ teaspoons pressed garlic
1 to 2 teaspoons sugar, or to taste

1 teaspoon salt
1 teaspoon cracked pepper
1 cup vegetable oil
60 to 80 asparagus spears, trimmed

Combine the vinegar, Dijon mustard, lemon juice, garlic, sugar, salt and pepper in a food processor and process until smooth. Add the oil gradually, processing constantly at high speed until creamy. Refrigerate, covered, until chilled.

Cook the asparagus in a large pot of boiling salted water for 3 to 5 minutes or just until fork-tender. Rinse under cold water; drain and pat dry with paper towels. Toss the asparagus with the vinaigrette. *Yield: 12 servings.*

NOTE: MAY ALSO SERVE THE VINAIGRETTE OVER MIXED GREENS.

Green Bean Bundles

$^3/_4$ cup packed brown sugar
$^1/_2$ cup (1 stick) butter, softened
2 teaspoons garlic powder

3 (14-ounce) cans whole green beans, drained
15 to 18 thin slices bacon

Heat the brown sugar, butter and garlic powder in a saucepan until the butter melts and the mixture forms a paste. Wrap 6 to 8 green beans at a time with $^1/_2$ to 1 slice bacon, securing with a wooden pick to form a bundle. Coat each bundle with some of the brown sugar paste. Place in two 9×13-inch baking pans. Bake at 350 degrees for 20 minutes. *Yield: 12 servings.*

Herbed Green Beans

1½ pounds fresh green beans, trimmed
1 cup (2 sticks) butter, softened
1 teaspoon marjoram
1 teaspoon rosemary, crushed

1 teaspoon thyme
⅛ teaspoon basil
⅛ teaspoon rubbed sage

Place a vegetable steamer in a large saucepan. Add 1 inch of water. Cover and bring to a boil. Uncover and add the green beans. Steam, covered, for about 8 minutes or until the beans are bright green and tender-crisp; drain.

Combine the butter, marjoram, rosemary, thyme, basil and sage in a bowl and mix well. Toss a desired amount of the herb butter with the green beans. (Refrigerate the remaining butter.) Garnish with dried cranberries. *Yield: 4 to 6 servings.*

Roasted Dill Green Beans

1 pound fresh green beans, trimmed
1 tablespoon olive oil
½ teaspoon salt
2 tablespoons white wine vinegar
2 teaspoons Dijon mustard
1 teaspoon fresh lemon juice

½ teaspoon sugar
½ teaspoon salt
½ teaspoon pepper
2 tablespoons olive oil
3 tablespoons chopped fresh dill weed

Combine the green beans, 1 tablespoon olive oil and ½ teaspoon salt in a roasting pan, tossing until the green beans are coated. Roast at 450 degrees for 20 to 30 minutes or until tender, stirring the green beans 3 times during roasting. Remove to a serving bowl.

Whisk the vinegar, Dijon mustard, lemon juice, sugar, salt and pepper in a small bowl, mixing well. Whisk in 2 tablespoons olive oil gradually. Pour over the green beans. Add the dill weed and toss to mix. Serve warm or at room temperature. *Yield: 4 servings.*

NOTE: THIS DISH IS GREAT SERVED WITH FISH, ESPECIALLY SALMON AND TUNA.

Pickled Brussels Sprouts

Kitchen Affairs

1 (10-ounce) package frozen brussels sprouts
1 cup white vinegar

$^3/_4$ cup sugar
$^1/_2$ cup prepared horseradish
$^1/_4$ teaspoon dry mustard

Combine the brussels sprouts, vinegar, sugar, horseradish and dry mustard in a sealable container. Marinate, covered, in the refrigerator for 8 to 12 hours or up to 1 week. Invert the container or mix thoroughly twice a day. Serve cold or at room temperature. *Yield: 3 servings.*

Copper Carrots

2 pounds carrots, sliced
1 small red bell pepper, chopped
1 medium onion, chopped
1 (10-ounce) can tomato soup
1 cup sugar

$^1/_2$ cup vegetable oil
$^1/_2$ cup vinegar
1 teaspoon dry mustard
1 teaspoon Worcestershire sauce
Salt and black pepper to taste

Cook the carrots in water to cover in a saucepan just until tender; do not overcook. Drain well, making sure all the steam has evaporated. Place the carrots in a bowl. Add the bell pepper, onion, tomato soup, sugar, oil, vinegar, dry mustard, Worcestershire sauce, salt and black pepper and mix well. Marinate, covered, in the refrigerator for several hours or up to 2 days. Serve cold. *Yield: 6 servings.*

Orange Ginger Carrots

8 medium carrots, cut diagonally into
1-inch slices
¼ cup orange juice
1 tablespoon sugar

1 teaspoon cornstarch
¼ teaspoon salt
¼ teaspoon ginger
1 tablespoon butter

Bring about 1 inch of lightly salted water to a boil in a 2-quart saucepan. Add the carrots. Cook, covered, for 10 to 15 minutes; drain. Return the carrots to the saucepan.

Combine the orange juice, sugar, cornstarch, salt and ginger in a small bowl. Pour over the carrots. Cook over low heat for 3 minutes, stirring constantly. Remove from the heat. Add the butter and toss gently to mix. *Yield: 4 servings.*

Kahlúa-Glazed Carrots

3 cups coarsely chopped carrots
1 tablespoon butter or margarine
1 tablespoon brown sugar
1 tablespoon honey
3 tablespoons Kahlúa or other
coffee-flavored liqueur

1 teaspoon cornstarch
¼ teaspoon salt
3 slices bacon, crisp-cooked, crumbled
1 tablespoon chopped fresh parsley

Place a vegetable steamer in a large saucepan. Add 1 inch of water. Cover and bring to a boil. Uncover and add the carrots. Steam, covered, for 4 to 5 minutes or until tender-crisp. Remove from the heat; set aside.

Melt the butter in a large skillet over medium heat. Stir in the brown sugar, honey and 2 tablespoons of the Kahlúa. Cook until bubbly. Combine the remaining 1 tablespoon Kahlúa and cornstarch in a bowl and mix well. Add to the honey mixture. Stir in the salt. Cook until thickened and bubbly. Add the carrots, tossing gently to coat. Cook just until the carrots are heated through. Spoon into a serving dish. Sprinkle with the bacon and parsley. *Yield: 6 servings.*

Couscous and Cabbage

3 tablespoons butter
1 small onion, coarsely chopped
1 small head cabbage, cut into strips

3 tablespoons sugar
1 (10-ounce) package plain couscous

Melt the butter in a 3-quart saucepan. Add the onion. Cook for 5 minutes. Add the cabbage. Cook, covered, for about 20 minutes or until the cabbage is wilted, stirring occasionally. Stir in the sugar. Cook for 2 to 3 minutes.

Prepare the couscous according to the package directions. Stir into the cabbage.
Yield: 6 to 8 servings.

Southern Indiana Corn Pudding

1 1/2 cups cream-style corn
1 cup yellow cornmeal
2 medium onions, chopped
3/4 cup buttermilk
1/2 cup (1 stick) butter, melted

2 eggs, beaten
1/2 teaspoon baking soda
1 1/2 to 2 cups (6 to 8 ounces) shredded
    sharp Cheddar cheese
1 (4-ounce) can diced green chiles

Combine the cream-style corn, cornmeal, onions, buttermilk, butter, eggs and baking soda in a large bowl and mix well. Pour 1/2 of the batter into a greased 9-inch square baking pan. Layer with 1/2 of the cheese, the green chiles and the remaining cheese and batter. Bake at 350 degrees for 1 hour. Cool in the pan for 15 minutes before cutting into squares. *Yield: 9 servings.*

NOTE: MAY BE PREPARED AHEAD AND CHILLED. BRING TO ROOM TEMPERATURE BEFORE BAKING.

Scalloped Corn Cake

1 (15-ounce) can whole kernel corn
1 (14-ounce) can cream-style corn
1 cup sour cream
$^1/_2$ cup (1 stick) margarine, melted
1 (8-ounce) package corn muffin mix
2 eggs
1 tablespoon sugar

Combine the whole kernel corn, cream-style corn, sour cream, margarine, muffin mix, eggs and sugar in a bowl. Pour into a greased 9×13-inch baking pan. Bake at 350 degrees for 45 minutes. *Yield*: 12 *servings*.

Stir-Fried Sugar Snap Peas

8 ounces fresh sugar snap peas
2 tablespoons vegetable oil
1 teaspoon dark sesame oil
3 tablespoons pine nuts
1 tablespoon minced fresh gingerroot
2 tablespoons dry sherry
2 tablespoons soy sauce

Snap the stems off the sugar snap peas, pulling down to remove the fibrous strings. Rinse the peas under running water; drain. Pat dry with paper towels.

Heat a heavy skillet over high heat. Add the vegetable oil and sesame oil, swirling the pan to mix. Add the pine nuts and gingerroot. Stir-fry until the pine nuts are light brown. Add the peas. Stir-fry to coat with oil. Stir in the sherry and soy sauce. Reduce the heat to medium. Cook, covered, for about 2 minutes or until heated through. Do not overcook; the peas should retain their crunch. *Yield*: 4 *servings*.

Stuffed Baby Eggplant

4 baby eggplants, or 2 small
eggplants, cut lengthwise
into halves
2 teaspoons coarse salt
1/4 cup olive oil
1 small onion, finely
chopped (1 cup)
1 small red bell pepper,
finely chopped (1 cup)
2 garlic cloves, minced

1/3 cup fresh bread crumbs
1/4 cup pine nuts, lightly
toasted
3 tablespoons raisins
3/4 cup (about 2 1/2 ounces)
freshly grated Kefalotyri
cheese or pecorino
cheese
1/4 cup fresh parsley leaves
Salt and black pepper to taste

Sprinkle the cut sides of the eggplant with the salt. Stand them in a
colander and drain for 30 minutes. Pat the eggplant dry with paper
towels. Heat the olive oil in a large heavy skillet over medium heat
until hot, but not smoking. Add the eggplant to the olive oil in
batches, cut side down. Cook for about 4 minutes or until the flesh
is golden brown and just tender. Turn the eggplant over. Cook for
1 minute. Remove to a plate and cool.

Pour off all but about 1 tablespoon of the olive oil from the
skillet. Add the onion. Sauté over medium-high heat for about
10 minutes or until golden brown, stirring frequently. Add the bell
pepper. Sauté until tender. Add the garlic. Sauté for 1 minute.
Remove to a large bowl to cool.

Scoop out the eggplant flesh, leaving 1/4-inch-thick shells in the
skins (do not puncture the shells). Place the shells in a shallow baking
dish that is just large enough to hold them in a single layer. Coarsely
chop the eggplant flesh. Stir into the onion mixture with the bread
crumbs, pine nuts, raisins, 1/2 cup of the cheese, parsley, salt and
black pepper. Spoon the eggplant mixture into the shells, mounding it
slightly. Sprinkle with the remaining 1/4 cup cheese. Bake at 375 degrees
for 20 minutes or until golden brown. Garnish with chopped fresh
parsley if desired. Serve warm or at room temperature. *Yield: 6 servings.*

NOTE: KEFALOTYRI CHEESE IS A HARD, YELLOW GREEK CHEESE MADE
FROM SHEEP'S MILK. STUFFED EGGPLANT MAY BE PREPARED **4** TO
6 HOURS IN ADVANCE, COVERED AND CHILLED BEFORE BAKING.

*Toasting heightens the flavor of
nuts, coconut, and sesame seeds.
To toast them, spread in a single
layer on a baking sheet. Bake at
350 degrees for 5 to 10 minutes
or until golden brown. Be sure
to watch them carefully in the
oven as they can burn easily.*

Fabulous Fried Onion Rings

Kitchen Affairs

1$\frac{1}{2}$ cups beer (warm or cold, flat or fresh)
1$\frac{1}{2}$ cups flour
3 or 4 jumbo-size yellow onions, cut into $\frac{1}{4}$-inch-thick slices
3 to 4 cups shortening
Salt to taste

Combine the beer and flour in a mixing bowl with an electric mixer or whisk and mix well. Cover the bowl loosely and let stand at room temperature for 3 to 12 hours.

Separate the onion slices into rings and let stand for 5 to 10 minutes. Remove and discard the inner transparent membrane from each onion ring using a fork, small pointed knife or fingernail. (Removing these membranes prevents the onion rings from shrinking during frying and pulling the batter away from the insides.)

Melt enough of the shortening in a large skillet to reach a 2-inch depth. Heat the melted shortening to 375 degrees. Dip the onion rings 1 at a time into the beer batter and lower gently into the hot shortening. Watch carefully to avoid hot splatters. Fry to an even golden brown color, turning as needed. Drain the onion rings on a baking sheet lined with several layers of paper towels or butcher paper. Keep warm in a 200-degree oven for up to 4 hours or until ready to serve. Season with salt and serve hot. *Yield: 6 to 8 servings.*

NOTE: MAY FREEZE AND REHEAT THE COOKED ONION RINGS. COOL THE ONION RINGS AND FREEZE THEM IN SEALABLE PLASTIC BAGS. REHEAT AT 400 DEGREES ON A BAKING SHEET FOR 4 TO 5 MINUTES.

My first experience of the Fall Festival was this year, and my most vivid memory is of "The Mouse Game." This game works a lot like roulette at a casino. You place a quarter on your favorite color or colors. The "dealer" spins the color wheel, which has a small box in the center. After a few rotations, the "dealer" opens the box and dumps out a real mouse. If the mouse runs and exits in your color, you win! Mind you, this is a real mouse! It's crazy!

Niki Traylor

Potatoes au Gratin

3 pounds white potatoes
6 shallots, chopped
2 to 4 tablespoons olive oil
Salt to taste

3 cups (12 ounces) shredded smoked
Gouda cheese
2 cups heavy cream

Slice the potatoes as thinly as possible with a mandoline or in a food processor fitted with a thin slicing disk; set aside.

Sauté the shallots in the olive oil in a skillet over medium heat for 20 minutes. Remove with a slotted spoon to paper towels; drain.

Arrange a single overlapping layer of potato slices in the bottom of a generously greased 9×9-inch baking dish. Season with salt. Top with some of the cheese and shallots and a small amount of the cream. Alternate layers of potatoes, salt, cheese, shallots and cream until all ingredients are used and the dish is full. Press on the top layer to release any air, especially in the center.

Bake at 375 degrees for 1½ to 1¾ hours or until the potatoes are tender. Cover with foil if the top begins to brown too quickly. Let stand, covered, for at least 30 minutes before serving. *Yield: 8 to 10 servings.*

Potatoes sto Fourno
(Lemon, Garlic and Oregano Roasted Potatoes)

3½ pounds russet potatoes, peeled,
cut into quarters
¼ cup olive oil
4 garlic cloves, chopped

1½ teaspoons oregano
Salt and pepper to taste
¼ cup fresh lemon juice
¼ cup water

Toss the potatoes with the olive oil, garlic, oregano, salt and pepper in a large nonreactive roasting pan. Spread the potatoes in a single layer. Pour the lemon juice and water over the potatoes. Roast at 425 degrees for about 45 minutes or until the potatoes are tender, stirring occasionally. *Yield: 8 servings.*

Twice-Baked Potato Casserole

8 potatoes, peeled, cooked and mashed
8 ounces cream cheese, softened
8 ounces sour cream
$^1/_2$ cup (1 stick) butter, softened
$^1/_2$ cup (2 ounces) shredded
    Cheddar cheese

1$^1/_2$ tablespoons minced onion
Dash of salt and pepper
6 slices bacon, crisp-cooked,
    crumbled
Additional shredded Cheddar cheese

Combine the potatoes, cream cheese, sour cream, butter, $^1/_2$ cup Cheddar cheese, onion, salt and pepper in a bowl. Spoon into a 2-quart baking dish. Bake at 350 degrees for 35 to 40 minutes. Sprinkle with the bacon and additional Cheddar cheese. Bake for 5 minutes. *Yield: 8 servings.*

Twice-Baked Potatoes

4 large Idaho potatoes
4 ounces cream cheese
2 tablespoons butter
1 teaspoon salt

1 teaspoon pepper
1 teaspoon dried minced onion
1 tablespoon milk
1 cup (4 ounces) shredded Cheddar cheese

Prick the potatoes in several places with a fork. Bake at 350 degrees for 1 to 1$^1/_4$ hours or until tender. Cool for 15 minutes. Cut the potatoes lengthwise into halves. Scoop the potato flesh into a bowl and mash, reserving the potato skins. Add the cream cheese, butter, salt, pepper and onion and mix well. Stir in milk as needed. The potatoes should be stiff.

    Use small pieces of foil to make "boats" to hold the reserved potato skins. Spoon the mashed potatoes into the skins. Bake at 350 degrees for 30 to 45 minutes, sprinkling the Cheddar cheese over the potatoes 15 minutes before removing them from the oven. *Yield: 4 servings.*

NOTE: MAY SUBSTITUTE 2 OUNCES SOUR CREAM AND 2 OUNCES CREAM CHEESE FOR THE 4 OUNCES CREAM CHEESE. MAY ALSO SPRINKLE CRUMBLED COOKED BACON OVER THE POTATOES.

Pumpkin Stuffed with Cranberry Compote

Evansville Living Magazine

1 whole pumpkin
(about 9 pounds)
1 tablespoon vegetable oil
2 cups sugar
1 cup packed brown sugar
1¼ cups apple cider
4 cups sliced peeled apples

2 cups fresh cranberries
2 cups pecan halves
1 cup golden raisins
8 ounces mixed dried fruit,
cut into large pieces (about
the size of a pecan half)
2 teaspoons pumpkin pie spice

Wash and dry the outside of the pumpkin. Cut out the top as for a jack-o'-lantern, making the opening large enough to easily fit a serving spoon. Reserve the lid. Scoop out the seeds and stringy membranes. Rinse the inside of the pumpkin with water; invert to drain.

Rub the outside of the pumpkin and its lid with the oil. Place the lid on the pumpkin and set in a large shallow baking pan that will hold it upright. Bake at 250 degrees for 1 hour.

Combine the sugar, brown sugar and cider in a large heavy saucepan. Cook over medium heat until the sugar is completely dissolved and the mixture comes to a boil, stirring frequently. Reduce the heat to low. Stir in the apples, cranberries, pecans, raisins, dried fruit and pumpkin pie spice. Remove from the heat.

Spoon the fruit mixture into the baked pumpkin, leaving at least 1 inch of headspace to prevent the fruit juices from bubbling over during baking. Replace the lid and cover the stem with foil to prevent burning. Bake at 250 degrees for 5 to 6 hours or until the pumpkin is soft, removing the lid carefully and stirring the filling 1 or 2 times during cooking. Pierce the pumpkin flesh near the top to test for tenderness. The pumpkin will be a beautiful burnished, crackled orange color.

Place the pumpkin on a decorative serving platter. Remove the lid and scoop out servings of fruit, scraping off a bit of pumpkin flesh with each serving. Serve warm or cooled with vanilla ice cream, whipped cream or sweetened heavy cream. *Yield: 12 servings.*

NOTE: FOR BEST RESULTS, SELECT A ROUND, SQUAT PUMPKIN WITH A FLAT BOTTOM.

Evansville, Indiana, is home to the fastest-growing city magazine in the United States—Evansville Living. Launched in March 2000, Evansville Living represents the dream of Todd and Kristen Tucker. They had never before published a city magazine but correctly believed that Evansville was ready for a glossy, colorful lifestyle magazine. Each bimonthly issue of Evansville Living highlights interesting local personalities, arts and entertainment, travel, homes and gardens, and local dining and menus. Evansville Living is committed to the community and is proud to have partnered with the Junior League of Evansville on several fund-raising events, including the biannual Evansville Living Idea Home.

Scalloped Rhubarb

4 cups sliced fresh rhubarb
1 cup sugar
5 dry dinner rolls, cut into
¾-inch cubes

½ cup sugar
1 teaspoon cinnamon
½ cup (1 stick) butter or margarine,
melted

Combine the rhubarb and 1 cup sugar in a saucepan. Cook until the rhubarb is mushy. Pour into a greased 9×13-inch baking dish. Top with the dinner roll cubes. Sprinkle with ½ cup sugar and the cinnamon. Drizzle with the butter. Bake at 350 degrees for 30 minutes. *Yield: 6 servings.*

Spinach Gratin

¼ cup (½ stick) unsalted butter
4 cups chopped yellow onions
(2 large)
¼ cup flour
¼ teaspoon nutmeg
2 cups milk
1 cup heavy cream

5 (10-ounce) packages frozen chopped
spinach, thawed, squeezed dry
1 cup (4 ounces) freshly grated Parmesan
cheese
Kosher salt to taste
½ teaspoon freshly ground pepper
½ cup (2 ounces) shredded Gruyère cheese

Melt the butter in a heavy sauté pan over medium heat. Add the onions. Sauté for about 15 minutes or until translucent. Add the flour and nutmeg. Cook for 2 minutes, stirring constantly. Stir in the milk and cream. Cook until thickened. Add the spinach and ½ cup of the Parmesan cheese and mix well. Season with salt and the pepper. Spoon the spinach mixture into a 1½-quart baking dish. Sprinkle with the remaining ½ cup Parmesan cheese and the Gruyère cheese. Bake at 425 degrees for 20 minutes or until hot and bubbly. Serve immediately. *Yield: 8 servings.*

Roasted Butternut Squash Risotto

A colorful side dish or vegetarian entrée

1 medium onion, chopped
2 tablespoons olive oil
1 tablespoon minced garlic
1 cup arborio rice
3 to 4 cups fat-free chicken broth, heated
2 cups (½-inch) roasted butternut squash pieces
3 cups fresh baby spinach, chopped
2 teaspoons chopped fresh sage
½ teaspoon cumin
3 tablespoons freshly grated Parmesan cheese
Salt and pepper to taste

Sauté the onion in the olive oil in a 5-quart saucepan for 5 minutes. Add the garlic and rice. Stir over low heat for 2 to 3 minutes. Add the hot chicken broth ½ cup at a time, simmering after each addition until the chicken broth is completely absorbed and stirring frequently. Continue adding the chicken broth until the rice has cooked for 25 to 30 minutes and is al dente, stirring frequently. Stir in the squash, spinach, sage, cumin and more chicken broth if the mixture appears dry. Stir gently over low heat until the spinach wilts. Remove from the heat. Stir in the cheese, salt and pepper. Serve immediately with additional Parmesan cheese. *Yield: 4 to 6 servings.*

NOTE: TO ROAST BUTTERNUT SQUASH, CUT 1 LARGE OR 2 SMALL BUTTERNUT SQUASH LENGTHWISE INTO HALVES. CUT EACH HALF CROSSWISE INTO 1½-INCH-WIDE PIECES. DRIZZLE WITH A LITTLE OLIVE OIL. ROAST SKIN SIDE DOWN AT 450 DEGREES FOR 40 TO 50 MINUTES; COOL. PEEL AND CUT INTO ½-INCH PIECES.

Arborio rice is a short grain rice that is traditionally used to make risotto. It has a high starch content that allows the grains to absorb the cooking liquid slowly, giving risotto its distinctive, creamy texture. Pearl rice may also be used to make risotto.

11

Sweet Potato Pudding

2 pounds sweet potatoes (about 4 or 5 medium)
3 eggs, lightly beaten
$^1/_2$ cup packed light brown sugar
$^1/_4$ cup milk
1 tablespoon flour
$^1/_2$ to1 teaspoon cinnamon
Brown sugar for sprinkling
Pecan halves

Boil or bake the sweet potatoes until soft; cool. Peel and set aside.

Combine the eggs, $^1/_2$ cup brown sugar, milk, flour and cinnamon in a large mixing bowl. Blend with an electric mixer until smooth. Add the sweet potatoes and mix well. Divide the sweet potato mixture evenly among 8 buttered $^1/_2$-cup ramekins. Sprinkle with brown sugar and place 1 to 2 pecan halves on top of each.

Place the ramekins on a baking sheet. Bake at 350 degrees for 25 to 30 minutes or until the tops begin to brown, the centers are set and the puddings are pulling away from the sides of the ramekins. Serve warm sprinkled with additional brown sugar and cinnamon if desired. *Yield: 8 servings.*

Basil Roasted Vegetables

3 zucchini, sliced crosswise $^1/_4$ inch thick
1 pound mushrooms, cut into halves
1 green bell pepper, cut into bite-size pieces
1 red bell pepper, cut into bite-size pieces
1 yellow bell pepper, cut into bite-size pieces
1 medium onion, cut into bite-size pieces
2 tablespoons chopped fresh basil
2 tablespoons balsamic vinegar
2 garlic cloves, minced
1 tablespoon olive oil
$^1/_2$ teaspoon salt
Blue cheese or feta cheese to taste

Combine the zucchini, mushrooms, bell peppers and onion in a bowl. Add the basil, vinegar, garlic, olive oil and salt. Toss well to coat the vegetables. Arrange in a single layer in a shallow roasting pan. Bake at 425 degrees for 35 minutes, crumbling cheese over the top during the last 5 minutes of baking. *Yield: 8 servings.*

At my first Fall Festival, I did not know what a brain sandwich was. I really thought it was chicken or something, because I ate a haystack and it was not hay! Well, anyway, I took a huge bite of this sandwich and asked my husband why it was mushy. He explained that it really was brain! I never spit so fast . . . !
Michelle Kerr Heuck

Ginger and Shiitake Mushroom Fried Rice

1 egg
1 tablespoon water
6 teaspoons (about) canola oil
6 to 8 scallions, white and green parts chopped separately
1½ teaspoons minced fresh gingerroot
¾ teaspoon kosher salt or sea salt
8 ounces fresh shiitake mushrooms, stems discarded,
caps thinly sliced
3 cups cooked rice
1 teaspoon sesame oil

Beat the egg with the water in a bowl. Warm a wok or large nonstick skillet over medium heat until hot. Add 1 teaspoon of the canola oil and swirl to coat the pan. Add ½ of the egg mixture and swirl to coat the bottom of the pan with a thin layer. Cook for about minute or until the egg is set. Remove the round of cooked egg from the pan. Add another teaspoon of the canola oil to the pan. Add the remaining egg mixture and repeat the cooking process. Stack the egg rounds and roll up like a cylinder. Cut the cylinder crosswise into small strips; set aside.

Heat the remaining 4 teaspoons canola oil in the wok over medium heat, adding more oil if needed to coat the pan. Add the white scallion parts, ginger and salt. Stir-fry for about 30 seconds. Add the mushrooms. Stir-fry for 3 to 5 minutes or until tender. Add the rice. Stir-fry for about 10 minutes or until the rice is light brown. Remove from the heat. Add the green scallion parts, egg strips and sesame oil and toss to mix. Taste and adjust the flavors by adding small amounts of salt and sesame oil. *Yield: 4 to 6 servings.*

Vermicelli Rice Casserole

6 tablespoons butter or margarine
4 ounces uncooked fine noodles
1 cup instant rice
1 cup chicken broth
1 cup French onion soup
$^1/_2$ cup water
$^1/_2$ teaspoon soy sauce

Melt the butter in a large skillet. Add the noodles. Sauté until golden brown, stirring frequently. Add the rice and stir to coat with the butter. Combine the noodle mixture, chicken broth, onion soup, water and soy sauce in a 2-quart baking dish. Bake, covered, at 350 degrees for 45 minutes. *Yield: 6 to 8 servings.*

Evansville is well known for its annual street food fest, the West Side Nut Club Fall Festival. I count down the days before I can indulge in a nice warm corn fritter soaked in maple syrup, or bite into a hand-dipped pronto pup from my favorite school booth. When I went away to college, my mom would UPS my favorites to me at school: the "big round one," a stromboli, and a sticky sugar-covered "monster ear." What a wonderful taste of home, even if it was soggy and a day old.

Melissa Singer

The Main Event

The Old Courthouse- A Downtown Landmark

If these walls could talk…what would they say? The Old Courthouse sits silently sphinx-like in downtown Evansville. Its elegant exterior belies the more colorful history of what lies within and below this landmark. The five stories that once housed Evansville's judicial system are now filled with local businesses, shops, and galleries. However, like people who once came here to plead their cases before a judge, this building also has quite a story to tell.

Outside, Indiana limestone surrounds the cornerstone of the Courthouse. At first glance it appears to be merely decorative; however, even the cornerstone has a secret. Embedded within it is a copper box that is carefully protected in a stone vault. When the cornerstone was laid in 1888, 100 carefully chosen items were placed inside the copper box. Some of the more interesting artifacts include a small shoe, a set of false teeth, photographs of the city, and a reward poster for a local embezzler. It is a treasure chest of sorts, as Evansvillians place great value on memories and tradition.

Far beneath the Courthouse, however, is where this story takes an unexpected turn. When the jail was built across the street from the Courthouse, an underground tunnel was constructed between the two buildings. Long ago, old jail guards wearily escorted various villains, gangsters, and convicts from the jail to the Courthouse and back again. This was the custom for many years. In the 1940s, however, there were several reports of missing prisoners and jailbreaks that have never been solved to this day. Legend has it that these crafty criminals escaped through the tunnel and vanished into the vast expanse of darkness under the Courthouse known as the Catacombs—never to be seen again! This legend inspired the Old Courthouse Catacombs Haunted House, which takes place each October and features a tour of the infamous tunnel.

From cornerstones to catacombs, the Old Courthouse remains a keeper of secrets. Future generations will continue to appreciate its beauty as well as remember what transpired between these walls…*once upon a time*.

Entrées

Elegant Mushroom-Stuffed Beef Tenderloin

8 ounces fresh mushrooms, sliced
$^1/_2$ cup chopped green onions
$^1/_4$ cup ($^1/_2$ stick) butter
$^1/_4$ cup chopped fresh parsley
1 (3-pound) whole beef tenderloin
1 teaspoon salt
1 teaspoon pepper
$^1/_2$ cup soy sauce
$^1/_3$ cup red wine
2 tablespoons brown sugar
2 tablespoons honey

Sauté the mushrooms and green onions in the butter in a skillet until tender; drain. Stir in the parsley; set aside.

Cut the tenderloin lengthwise, cutting to but not through the bottom. Sprinkle with the salt and pepper. Spoon the mushroom mixture into the opening. Tie the tenderloin with kitchen string or unwaxed dental floss to help retain its shape during roasting. Place the tenderloin in a baking dish.

Combine the soy sauce, wine, brown sugar and honey in a bowl. Pour over the tenderloin. Refrigerate, covered, for 8 to 12 hours.

Remove the tenderloin from the marinade; discard the marinade or reserve for sauce (see Note). Place the tied tenderloin on a rack in a roasting pan. Roast at 425 degrees for 30 to 40 minutes or until the tenderloin registers 145 degrees on a meat thermometer for medium-rare, 160 degrees for medium or to desired doneness. Let stand for 10 minutes before removing the string and serving. *Yield: 6 to 8 servings.*

NOTE: FOR A DELICIOUS SAUCE, DOUBLE THE MUSHROOM MIXTURE AND RESERVE HALF. COMBINE WITH RESERVED MARINADE. BRING TO A BOIL FOR ONE MINUTE AND SERVE WITH THE TENDERLOIN.

Fabulous Beef Tenderloin

1 (4- to 5-pound) beef
tenderloin, trimmed
2 tablespoons unsalted
butter

1 tablespoon coarse salt
1 tablespoon cracked pepper

Place the tenderloin on a foil-lined baking sheet. Slather evenly with the butter. Sprinkle with the salt and pepper. Roast at 500 degrees for 22 minutes for rare, 25 minutes for medium-rare or until a meat thermometer registers 145 to 160 degrees. Remove from the oven and cover tightly with foil. Let stand for 20 minutes. Remove the string and cut into thick slices. *Yield: 8 to 10 servings.*

Sauerbraten

2 cups cider vinegar
1 cup red wine (optional)
1 cup water
$^1/_2$ cup sugar
3 small bay leaves
2 teaspoons salt
2 teaspoons ground pepper
1 teaspoon whole
peppercorns

1 teaspoon whole cloves
1 teaspoon mustard seeds
$^1/_2$ teaspoon ground allspice
1 (4- to 6-pound)
eye-of-round roast
1 lemon, cut into $^1/_4$-inch
slices
Gingersnap cookies, crushed

Combine the first 11 ingredients in a saucepan. Bring to a boil. Pour the hot vinegar mixture over the roast in a large heatproof bowl. Cool completely. Add the lemon slices. Marinate, covered, in the refrigerator for 4 days, turning the roast daily.

Remove the roast from the marinade, straining and reserving the marinade. Drain the roast thoroughly. Brown the roast slowly in a Dutch oven. Add 2 cups of the reserved marinade. Roast at 350 degrees for 30 minutes. Cover the pan. Braise in the oven for 3 hours.

Bring the remaining reserved marinade to a boil in a saucepan. Boil for 1 minute. Stir in enough crushed gingersnap cookies to thicken the gravy, heating thoroughly. *Yield: 8 to 10 servings.*

Horseradish Salsa

For big flavor in a flash, mix up this zesty salsa! It's a quick and easy addition to pork or beef tenderloin.

1 (16-ounce) jar salsa
$^1/_2$ cup loosely packed fresh parsley leaves, chopped
2 tablespoons white horseradish

Combine the salsa, parsley and horseradish in a bowl and mix well. Chill, covered, for up to 2 hours. Bring to room temperature before serving.

22

Italian Meat Loaf

1 cup boiling water	½ cup (2 ounces) shredded sharp
½ cup dry-pack sun-dried tomatoes	provolone cheese
1 pound ground round	½ cup ketchup
1 cup seasoned bread crumbs	2 egg whites
¾ cup finely chopped white onion	2 garlic cloves, minced
¾ cup chopped fresh basil	⅓ cup ketchup

Combine the boiling water and sun-dried tomatoes in a bowl. Let stand for 30 minutes or until the tomatoes are soft; drain. Finely chop the tomatoes; set aside.

Combine the ground round, bread crumbs, onion, basil, cheese, ½ cup ketchup, egg whites and garlic in a large bowl. Add the sun-dried tomatoes. Shape the meat mixture into a 5×9-inch loaf on a broiler pan coated with nonstick cooking spray. Spread ⅓ cup ketchup over the top of the meat loaf.

Bake at 350 degrees for 1 hour or until a meat thermometer registers 160 degrees. Let stand for 10 minutes before slicing. Cut into 12 slices. Serve with your favorite mashed potatoes if desired. *Yield: 6 servings.*

French Dip Sandwiches

1 (3½- to 4-pound) boneless	1 teaspoon rosemary
chuck roast, trimmed	1 teaspoon garlic powder
½ cup soy sauce	3 or 4 peppercorns
⅓ cup barbecue sauce (optional)	1 bay leaf
1 beef bouillon cube	6 to 8 French rolls, split
1 teaspoon thyme	

Place the roast in a 5-quart slow cooker. Combine the soy sauce, barbecue sauce, bouillon cube, thyme, rosemary, garlic powder, peppercorns and bay leaf in a bowl. Pour over the roast. Add enough water to cover the roast. Cook on Low for 7 hours or until tender.

Remove the roast from the slow cooker. Strain and reserve the cooking broth. Shred the roast with a fork. Place the shredded roast on the rolls and serve with the broth for dipping. *Yield: 6 to 8 servings.*

NOTE: GREAT SERVED WITH GRILLED ONIONS AND PEPPERS.

Honey Grilled Pork Tenderloin

2 (12-ounce) pork tenderloins	2 tablespoons brown sugar
$1/4$ cup soy sauce	3 tablespoons honey
5 garlic cloves, minced	2 teaspoons dark sesame oil
$1/2$ teaspoon ginger	

Make a lengthwise cut down the center of each tenderloin, cutting to within $1/4$ inch of the opposite side. Open the tenderloins, pressing to flatten them.

Combine the soy sauce, garlic and ginger in a shallow dish. Add the tenderloins. Chill, covered, for 3 hours, turning the tenderloins occasionally.

Combine the brown sugar, honey and sesame oil in a bowl; set aside. Remove the tenderloins from the marinade; discard the marinade. Grill, covered, over medium-hot coals for 20 minutes or until a meat thermometer inserted into the thickest portion of the tenderloin registers 160 degrees, turning occasionally and basting with the honey mixture. Let stand for 10 minutes before carving. *Yield: 6 servings.*

124

Cranberry Pork Roast

1 ($2^1/2$- to 3-pound) boneless rolled pork loin roast	1 teaspoon dry mustard
1 (16-ounce) can jellied cranberry sauce	$1/4$ teaspoon cloves
$1/2$ cup sugar	2 tablespoons cornstarch
$1/2$ cup cranberry juice	2 tablespoons cold water
	Salt to taste

Place the roast in a slow cooker. Mash the cranberry sauce in a medium bowl. Stir in the sugar, cranberry juice, dry mustard and cloves. Pour over the roast. Cook on Low for 6 to 8 hours or until tender. Remove the roast from the slow cooker; keep warm.

Skim the fat from the cooking juices. Measure 2 cups cooking juices, adding water if necessary. Pour into a saucepan. Bring to a boil over medium-high heat. Combine the cornstarch and cold water in a bowl to make a paste. Stir into the hot juices. Cook until thickened, stirring constantly. Season with salt. Serve with the sliced roast. *Yield: 6 to 8 servings.*

Pork Tenderloin with Jezebel Sauce

Jezebel Sauce
1 (12-ounce) jar pineapple preserves
1 (10-ounce) jar apple jelly
$^1/_4$ cup Dijon mustard
2 tablespoons prepared horseradish

Herb Marinade
1 cup soy sauce
2 tablespoons fresh lemon juice
1 tablespoon finely chopped garlic
1 tablespoon chopped fresh chives
2 teaspoons chopped fresh tarragon
2 teaspoons chopped fresh basil
1 teaspoon ground sage
1 teaspoon pepper
3 to 4 pounds pork tenderloin

For the Jezebel sauce, combine the pineapple preserves, apple jelly, Dijon mustard and horseradish in a small bowl and mix well. Refrigerate, covered, for up to 1 month. Bring to room temperature before serving.

For the herb marinade, combine the soy sauce, lemon juice, garlic, chives, tarragon, basil, sage and pepper in a small bowl. Place the pork in a shallow dish. Pour the marinade over the pork. Marinate, tightly covered, for 30 minutes at room temperature or for 8 to 12 hours in the refrigerator, turning the pork several times.

Remove the pork from the marinade, reserving the marinade. Place the pork in a shallow roasting pan. Roast at 325 degrees for 15 to 20 minutes per pound or until a meat thermometer registers 160 degrees, basting with the reserved marinade. Do not baste during the last 5 minutes of roasting. Discard any remaining marinade. Let stand for 10 minutes before carving. Serve with Jezebel Sauce.
Yield: 8 to 10 servings.

Bourbon Marinade
Evansville Living Magazine

Whisk $^1/_2$ cup chives or green onion tops, $^1/_4$ to $^1/_2$ cup packed dark brown sugar, $^1/_4$ cup Dijon mustard, $^1/_4$ cup bourbon, 2 tablespoons Worcestershire sauce and $^1/_4$ cup soy sauce in a bowl. Use to marinate pork or chicken for up to 8 hours or shrimp for up to 4 hours.

For best results and ease of cleanup, marinate meats and seafood in a large sealable plastic bag, turning the bag and gently massaging the food inside every few hours. Marinades should be discarded after the meat or seafood is removed unless they will be used as sauces.

For proper food safety, boil marinades for 3 to 5 minutes before serving alongside the cooked meat or seafood.

Pork Tenderloin with
Sherry Mushroom Sauce

Unsure just how long

to cook your meat? Enlist the

aid of a meat thermometer,

which guarantees perfectly

cooked meat every time. To use,

insert the thermometer

into the center of the thickest

portion of the meat, taking

care to avoid a bone or fat. If

it has reached the desired

temperature, remove it from the

oven and let it stand a few

minutes before carving. Always

remember that meat continues

to cook while standing.

Sherry Marinade
3 to 4 pounds pork tenderloin
Soy sauce
Water
³/₄ cup cream sherry
¹/₂ cup vegetable oil
¹/₃ cup toasted sesame seeds
10 green onions, sliced
2 garlic cloves, minced

Sauce
3 tablespoons butter
1¹/₂ pounds brown, button or portobello mushrooms, sliced
4 shallots, sliced
1 pint heavy cream
1 cup cream sherry
Salt and pepper to taste

For *the sherry marinade*, place the pork in a shallow dish. Cover the pork with equal amounts of soy sauce and water. Stir in the sherry, oil, sesame seeds, green onions and garlic. Marinate, covered, in the refrigerator for 8 to 12 hours.

For *the sauce*, melt the butter in a skillet. Add the mushrooms and shallots. Sauté until tender. Add the heavy cream, sherry, salt and pepper. Stir over medium-low heat until slightly thickened; keep warm.

Remove the pork from the marinade; discard the marinade. Grill the pork until a meat thermometer registers 160 degrees. Let stand for 10 minutes before carving. Serve with the sauce. *Yield: 8 to 10 servings.*

Pork Medallions with Blackberry Sauce

2 (1-pound) pork tenderloins
1 teaspoon salt
1 teaspoon coarsely ground pepper
1 teaspoon ground allspice
2 tablespoons butter

$^{1}/_{2}$ cup coarsely chopped shallots
$^{2}/_{3}$ cup dry white wine
2 tablespoons seedless blackberry jam
2 tablespoons butter

Sprinkle the pork with the salt, pepper and allspice. Refrigerate, covered, for 30 minutes.

Grill the pork over medium-hot coals for 20 minutes or until a meat thermometer registers 160 degrees, turning once. Let stand for 10 minutes before slicing.

Melt 2 tablespoons butter in a small saucepan over medium-high heat. Add the shallots. Sauté for 5 minutes or until tender. Stir in the wine. Cook for 13 minutes or until the liquid is reduced by half. Reduce the heat to low. Whisk in the jam and 2 tablespoons butter. Cook for 2 minutes or until slightly thickened.

Cut the pork into $^{1}/_{4}$-inch-thick slices. Drizzle with the blackberry sauce. Garnish with fresh blackberries and fresh thyme sprigs. *Yield: 6 servings.*

Garlic Spareribs

2 to 3 pounds spareribs, cut into
1$^{1}/_{2}$-inch portions
Salt and pepper to taste
1 cup water

$^{3}/_{4}$ cup packed light brown sugar
3 tablespoons soy sauce
1 garlic clove, cut into slivers
$^{1}/_{4}$ teaspoon ginger

Season the spareribs with salt and pepper. Cook in a dry skillet until brown. Combine the water, brown sugar, soy sauce, garlic and ginger in a large pot. Bring to a simmer. Add the browned ribs. Simmer slowly for about 1 hour or until the ribs are tender and cooked through. (If the sauce becomes too thick during simmering, add water to prevent scorching.) *Yield: 4 to 6 servings.*

Pork Tacos

1 tablespoon olive oil
1/2 cup chopped onion
1/2 cup chopped green bell pepper
1 teaspoon minced garlic
2 tablespoons olive oil
2 pounds pork tenderloin
Salt, black pepper and olive oil to taste

1 (8-ounce) can tomato sauce
1/2 cup dry red wine
1 teaspoon cumin
1 teaspoon chili powder
1 bay leaf
1/2 teaspoon salt
Flour tortillas, warmed

Heat 1 tablespoon olive oil in a large sauté pan over medium heat. Add the onion, bell pepper and garlic. Cook until tender. Remove from the pan and set aside.

Heat 2 tablespoons olive oil in the same pan over medium-high heat. Season the pork by rubbing salt, black pepper and olive oil into the surface. Add to the hot oil. Cook until brown on all sides. Return the onion mixture to the pan. Add the tomato sauce, wine, cumin, chili powder, bay leaf and 1/2 teaspoon salt. Reduce the heat to medium-low. Simmer for 30 to 60 minutes or until the pork is tender and cooked through. Remove and discard the bay leaf.

Remove the pork from the pan. Shred with 2 forks. Return the shredded pork to the pan and mix well. Serve in warm tortillas with assorted toppings (such as shredded cheese, sour cream, black olives and shredded lettuce). *Yield: 6 to 8 servings.*

Slovakian Pigs

1 pound ground sirloin
8 ounces Italian sausage,
    casings removed
1 cup cooked rice
1 large green bell pepper,
    coarsely chopped

1/4 cup chopped onion
Dash of salt
Dash of black pepper
2 large heads green cabbage
1 (15-ounce) can tomato sauce
1 (15-ounce) can whole tomatoes

Combine the ground sirloin, sausage, rice, bell pepper, onion, salt and black pepper in a bowl; set aside. Pull off whole leaves from the cabbage heads and rinse under cold water. Cook in boiling salted water in a saucepan until tender and dark green; drain. Stack the leaves on a plate.

Roll the ground sirloin mixture into small balls. Place each meatball on a cabbage leaf and roll up to enclose, securing the leaf with a wooden pick. Place the cabbage rolls in a large pot. Add the tomato sauce and tomatoes. Bring to a boil. Reduce the heat to low. Simmer for 40 to 60 minutes or until the meatballs are cooked through, stirring occasionally. *Yield: 6 to 8 servings.*

Pulled Pork Barbecue with Mop Sauce and Shoulder Dry Rub

The Flying Pigs Barbecue Team

Mop Sauce

2 cups cider vinegar	3 tablespoons paprika
1 1/2 cups vegetable oil	2 tablespoons garlic salt
Juice of 1 lemon	1 tablespoon onion powder

Dry Rub

3/4 cup paprika	1 tablespoon chili powder
1/3 cup garlic salt	2 teaspoons dry mustard
1/3 cup onion salt	2 teaspoons cayenne pepper
1/4 cup salt	1 teaspoon oregano
2 tablespoons brown sugar	1 teaspoon cumin

Pork

1 (4- to 7-pound) pork butt	Barbecue sauce

For the mop sauce, combine the vinegar, oil, lemon juice, paprika, garlic salt and onion powder in a bowl; set aside.

For the dry rub, combine the paprika, garlic salt, onion salt, salt, brown sugar, chili powder, dry mustard, cayenne pepper, oregano and cumin in a bowl or jar and mix well. Dust all sides of the pork butt liberally with the rub mixture. Cover the pork with plastic wrap. Refrigerate for 1 to 12 hours.

Bring the pork to room temperature. Soak wood chips for grilling (preferably a mix of 2 or more types of wood: hickory, apple, cherry, oak or persimmon) in water. Prepare a charcoal grill for indirect cooking with hot coals on 1 side of the grill and the soaked wood chips on the other side. Place the pork over the wood chips. Grill, covered, for 1 hour. Baste with the mop sauce. Continue grilling for 5 to 7 hours or until a meat thermometer registers 170 degrees, basting every 45 minutes with the mop sauce. (It may be necessary to add more coals during cooking.) Baste the pork liberally with your favorite barbecue sauce. Grill, covered, for 15 minutes. (The pork will develop a dark outer layer referred to as bark.)

Remove the pork from the grill. Tear the pork into pieces with a knife and fork or 2 forks. Serve on buns topped with barbecue sauce and coleslaw. *Yield: 10 to 12 servings.*

Champagne Mustard

1 1/2 cups sugar

15 tablespoons dry mustard

3 tablespoons flour

1 1/2 teaspoons salt

1 1/2 teaspoons pepper

6 eggs, beaten

3/4 cup vinegar

3/4 cup Champagne

3 tablespoons butter

Combine the sugar, dry mustard, flour, salt and pepper in the top of a double boiler. Whisk the eggs, vinegar and Champagne together in a bowl. Add to the mustard mixture. Place over simmering water. Cook until thickened, stirring occasionally. Add the butter and stir until melted. Pour into jars. Store in the refrigerator for up to 1 month.
Yield: about 1 quart

Apple Butter Ham

1 (8- to 10-pound) fully cooked ham
24 whole cloves
1 (15-ounce) jar apple butter
1 1/2 cups ginger ale
1 cup maple syrup
1/2 cup brown mustard

Score the fat on the ham into a diamond design. Stud the scored fat with the cloves. Place the ham fat side up in a lightly greased 9×13-inch baking dish. Combine the apple butter, ginger ale, maple syrup and brown mustard in a bowl. Pour evenly over the ham.
　　Bake at 350 degrees on the lower oven rack for 2 1/2 hours, basting with pan juices every 15 to 20 minutes. *Yield: 20 servings.*

Game Day Sandwiches

1 pound shaved ham
1/4 cup (1/2 stick) butter or margarine, melted
2 tablespoons poppy seeds
2 tablespoons mustard
2 tablespoons Worcestershire sauce
8 hamburger buns
8 slices Swiss cheese

Combine the ham, butter, poppy seeds, mustard and Worcestershire sauce in a bowl. Spread on the buns. Top with the cheese slices. Wrap each sandwich individually in foil. Bake at 350 degrees for 10 to 15 minutes or until the cheese melts. *Yield: 8 servings.*

Brain Sandwiches

Brain sandwiches are a tradition at Evansville's Annual West Side Nut Club Fall Festival. Lines for this festival favorite are usually about an hour long! Brain sandwiches are to Evansville what sourdough bread is to San Francisco!

12 ounces (about) cleaned pork brains
3 to 4 tablespoons (heaping) flour
1 teaspoon baking powder
1 egg
Salt and pepper to taste
Vegetable oil for frying
6 to 8 hamburger buns

Wash the brains in pieces under cold running water, removing as much of the thin membrane as possible. Knead the brains with your hands to break them into small lumps. Combine the brains, flour, baking powder, egg, salt and pepper in a large mixing bowl. Beat at medium-low speed until nearly smooth. (Some lumps will remain in the batter.)

Pour oil into a skillet to a ¼-inch depth. Heat until hot but not smoking. Drop about 3 tablespoons of the batter at a time into the oil. Fry for 5 minutes or until the batter bubbles and begins to look dry. Turn and fry for 5 minutes longer or until the edges are crispy and golden brown. Serve on the buns with burger-type accompaniments. *Yield: 6 to 8 servings.*

The food that most typifies Evansville is "barbecue." Moving here from Chicago, I had never heard of "barbecue." I always thought that barbecue was when you had people over and you grilled out. Between Shyler's and Wolf's, Evansville has the best barbecue around! (The barbecue recipes at both Shyler's and Wolf's are such closely guarded secrets that we couldn't share them in this cookbook—you'll just have to visit Evansville and try them for yourself!)

Heather King

131

The Flying Pigs (Mike Ball, Mike Gieneart, Chad Klenck, Kirk Knight, Burkley McCarthy, Chris Mills, Mike Richardson, Carter Stegall, Mike Stepto, Robert Woosley, Chris Wright, and Joe Wright) were formed in 1991 in Memphis, Tennessee. When one of its founders, Chris Mills, moved to Evansville in 1995, he introduced his new friends to the "sport" of barbecue. This group competes in many contests around the country, including the Memphis in May World Barbecue Championship. The Flying Pigs have won numerous awards, including the honor of being named two-time Illinois State Rib Champions and taking 1st Place Pork Shoulder at the World Championship. For more information, visit www.flyingpigsbbq.com.

Grilled Leg of Lamb

The Flying Pigs Barbecue Team

$^2/_3$ cup chopped fresh mint
$^1/_4$ cup olive oil
4 garlic cloves, minced
1 tablespoon salt (preferably kosher)
2 teaspoons cumin
$1^1/_2$ teaspoons coriander
1 teaspoon black pepper
1 teaspoon cayenne pepper
1 teaspoon fresh lemon juice
1 (6-pound) butterflied leg of lamb, or 1 (9-pound) bone-in leg of lamb

Combine the mint, olive oil, garlic, salt, cumin, coriander, black pepper, cayenne pepper and lemon juice in a bowl. Let the marinade stand for 15 minutes. Place the lamb in a baking dish. Pour the marinade over the lamb, coating evenly. Cover with plastic wrap. Marinate in the refrigerator until ready to grill.

Prepare a charcoal grill for indirect cooking with hot coals on 1 side of the grill. Remove the lamb from the marinade; discard the marinade. Place the lamb on the grill but not over the coals. Grill, covered, for 45 to 60 minutes or until a meat thermometer registers 145 degrees for rare. Let stand for 10 minutes before carving. Serve with mint jelly if desired. *Yield: 16 servings.*

NOTE: THIS MARINADE ALSO WORKS WELL WITH LAMB CHOPS. THE LAMB MAY ALSO BE INFUSED WITH GARLIC BEFORE MARINATING BY MAKING SMALL INCISIONS WITH THE TIP OF A KNIFE AND INSERTING ROASTED GARLIC CLOVES.

Eastern Mediterranean Lamb and Bulgur Loaf

1 cup canned crushed
    tomatoes
1/3 cup medium-grain bulgur
1/4 cup olive oil
2 cups finely chopped onions
6 garlic cloves, minced
2 1/2 pounds lean
    ground lamb

2 eggs, beaten
2 teaspoons salt
1 1/2 teaspoons pepper
16 ounces plain yogurt
3 tablespoons fresh lemon
    juice
1/2 teaspoon salt

Combine the tomatoes and bulgur in a small bowl. Let stand for 30 minutes, stirring once or twice.

Heat the olive oil in a large skillet over medium heat. Add the onions and garlic. Cook, covered, for 10 minutes, stirring once or twice. Remove from the heat; cool completely.

Combine the ground lamb, bulgur mixture, onion mixture, eggs, 2 teaspoons salt and the pepper in a large bowl and mix well. Remove to a shallow baking dish and shape into a flat loaf about 2 1/2 inches thick. Smooth the top of the loaf with the back of a spoon.

Bake at 350 degrees for about 1 hour and 10 minutes or until a meat thermometer registers 145 degrees. Let stand on a rack until cool.

Whisk the yogurt, lemon juice and 1/2 teaspoon salt together in a small bowl. Slice the meat loaf and spoon some of the yogurt sauce over each piece. *Yield: 8 to 10 servings.*

NOTE: THIS LOAF TAKES ITS INSPIRATION FROM THE MIDDLE EASTERN DISH KIBBEH, WHICH COMBINES RAW LAMB AND BULGUR (A PARBOILED QUICK-COOKING CRACKED WHEAT). BAKING THESE TWO INGREDIENTS TOGETHER TRANSFORMS THEM INTO SOMETHING COMPLETELY AMERICAN. MAY PREPARE THE MEAT LOAF A DAY AHEAD AND STORE, COVERED, IN THE REFRIGERATOR. BRING TO ROOM TEMPERATURE BEFORE SERVING. MAY ADD CHOPPED FRESH PARSLEY TO THE YOGURT SAUCE FOR EXTRA COLOR.

Marinated Cucumber and Tomato Salad

1/2 cup white vinegar

1/4 cup sugar

1/4 cup olive oil

2 tablespoons chopped fresh mint

1 1/2 teaspoons salt

1/4 teaspoon pepper

3 medium cucumbers, peeled,
cut into 1/4-inch slices

3 medium tomatoes,
cut into wedges

1 medium red onion,
thinly sliced

Whisk the vinegar, sugar, olive oil, mint, salt and pepper in a large bowl. Add the cucumbers, tomatoes and onion, tossing gently to coat. Chill, covered, for at least 2 hours.

Yield: 8 servings

Roulade of Chicken Rustica Heironimus

Oak Meadow Golf Club, Inc. Pam Heironimus, Executive Chef

Almost all of my food memories come from my Gram, Julia Clutter. She's the greatest cook in the world. No one makes better fried chicken. She rarely makes it anymore, though, because her electric skillet stopped working. She said it was the best kind of skillet for making the chicken because the heating element covered the whole bottom of the pan rather than just a circle like the new electric skillets. My husband and I have searched high and low for such a skillet. We go to rummage sales and flea markets, but we haven't found one yet. She'll still make the chicken if we beg . . . maybe once a year. No matter what kind of skillet she uses, it's still just as good even if she thinks it isn't!

Andi Miller

34

4 boneless skinless chicken breast halves, butterflied
Kosher salt and cracked black peppercorns to taste
$\frac{1}{4}$ cup ($\frac{1}{2}$ stick) butter, melted
4 thin slices prosciutto
4 tablespoons ($\frac{1}{4}$ cup) prepared pesto
4 ounces mozzarella cheese, shredded
2 roasted red bell peppers, cut into halves
Alfredo sauce or marinara sauce

Pound the chicken between sheets of plastic wrap until uniformly thin. Sprinkle with salt and black peppercorns on both sides. Position each piece with the tendon (where the halves were joined) pointing directly toward you. Brush with some of the melted butter. Layer 1 prosciutto slice, 1 tablespoon pesto, 1 ounce cheese and 1 roasted pepper half on each chicken piece. Press the layers together gently with the back of a large spoon or the palm of your hand. Roll up the chicken, beginning with the tendon end. Secure the rolls with wooden picks or kitchen string.

Place the chicken rolls seam side down on a parchment-lined baking sheet. Brush with the remaining melted butter. Bake at 350 degrees for 30 to 35 minutes or until the chicken is cooked through. Let stand for 5 to 10 minutes.

Trim off the ends of each roll (roulade) to achieve a uniform end. Slice each roulade crosswise into $\frac{1}{2}$-inch pieces. Serve the roulade slices fanned over your favorite marinara or Alfredo sauce. Yield: 4 *servings.*

Chicken Breasts Florentine

Kennel Club of Evansville

4 (6-ounce) boneless chicken breasts
1 (14-ounce) can chicken broth
1 pint heavy cream
1/2 cup (2 ounces) grated Parmesan cheese
Salt and pepper to taste
1 small onion, chopped
8 ounces fresh button mushrooms, thinly sliced
2 tablespoons vegetable oil
2 ounces fresh spinach leaves

Place the chicken in a baking dish. Bake at 350 degrees for about 15 minutes or until cooked through; keep warm.

Heat the chicken broth in a saucepan until reduced by half. Add the cream and heat through. Stir in the cheese gradually, stirring until completely melted. Season with salt and pepper; set aside.

Sauté the onion and mushrooms in the oil in a skillet until tender. Stir into the cream sauce along with the spinach. Heat for 3 minutes over low heat. Spoon over the warm chicken. *Yield: 4 servings.*

NOTE: SERVE WITH A CHARDONNAY OR SAUVIGNON BLANC.

The Kennel Club of Evansville was created in 1925 as a sporting club for area dog breeders. Dog trials were held on several dates each year. The club was incorporated in 1945, the same year the first clubhouse was built. Today, the Kennel Club is a private dining facility featuring classic American and European cuisine. It is well known for its fine food and casual, yet elegant, atmosphere amid a relaxing countryside setting.

135

Garlic Chicken

2 cups sour cream
2 tablespoons lemon juice
4 garlic cloves, minced
4 teaspoons celery salt
4 teaspoons Worcestershire sauce
2 teaspoons paprika

$^{1}/_{2}$ teaspoon pepper
8 boneless skinless chicken breasts
2 cups crushed butter crackers
  (about 5 cups whole crackers)
$^{1}/_{2}$ cup (1 stick) butter, melted
$^{1}/_{4}$ cup vegetable oil

Combine the sour cream, lemon juice, garlic, celery salt, Worcestershire sauce, paprika and pepper in a large shallow glass dish. Add the chicken, turning to coat both sides. Refrigerate, covered, for 3 to 4 hours.

   Place the cracker crumbs in a shallow bowl. Roll the chicken in the crumbs to coat. Arrange in a greased 9×13-inch baking dish. Combine the butter and oil. Pour over the chicken. Bake at 350 degrees for 50 to 60 minutes or until the chicken is cooked through. *Yield: 8 servings.*

Bella Braised Chicken

1 tablespoon margarine
2 medium onions, chopped (1$^{1}/_{2}$ cups)
2 ribs celery, coarsely chopped
  (1$^{1}/_{2}$ cups)
1 large carrot, coarsely chopped (1 cup)
2 garlic cloves, minced
3 tablespoons flour
$^{1}/_{4}$ teaspoon pepper

6 (4-ounce) boneless skinless chicken
  breasts, pounded
1 tablespoon olive oil
1 (14-ounce) can diced tomatoes
1 cup chicken broth
$^{1}/_{2}$ cup dry white wine
2 tablespoons minced parsley
1 teaspoon thyme

Melt the margarine in a large nonstick skillet. Add the onions, celery, carrot and garlic. Cook for about 5 minutes or until soft, stirring occasionally. Remove the vegetables to a 3-quart baking dish; set aside.

   Combine the flour and pepper in a 1-gallon sealable plastic bag. Add the chicken and shake to coat. Heat the olive oil in the same skillet. Add the chicken. Cook for 2 minutes on each side or until brown. Arrange the chicken over the vegetables in the baking dish.

   Combine the tomatoes, chicken broth, wine, parsley and thyme in the skillet. Heat to a boil, scraping up any browned bits. Pour over the chicken.

   Bake, covered, at 325 degrees for about 1 hour or until the chicken is cooked through and the vegetables are tender. *Yield: 6 servings.*

Lemon Chicken

1 egg white
2 tablespoons sesame oil
1 tablespoon cornstarch
2 teaspoons chopped garlic
$^1/_4$ teaspoon white pepper
5 boneless skinless chicken breasts, cut into 1-inch cubes
1 tablespoon olive oil or canola oil
3 tablespoons fresh lemon juice
2 tablespoons soy sauce
$1^1/_2$ tablespoons sugar
Hot cooked jasmine rice

Combine the egg white, sesame oil, cornstarch, garlic and white pepper in a sealable plastic bag. Add the chicken; seal the bag. Marinate in the refrigerator for at least 2 hours.

Heat the olive oil in a skillet. Add the chicken, discarding the marinade. Sauté until brown.

Combine the lemon juice, soy sauce and sugar in a bowl. Pour over the chicken in the skillet, stirring to coat. Bring to a simmer. Remove to a serving platter. Serve with the jasmine rice.
Yield: 5 servings.

Basmati and jasmine rices are both aromatic, long grain rices often used in Thai and Indian dishes. Many cooks prefer them because of their mild, yet distinctive, nutty flavor.

137

Chicken Marbella

3/4 cup dried apricots
3/4 cup pitted large green olives
1/4 cup olive oil
1/4 cup red wine vinegar
2 tablespoons oregano
2 tablespoons capers
5 large garlic cloves, minced
3 bay leaves
Coarse (kosher) salt and freshly ground pepper to taste
6 large boneless chicken breasts
1/2 cup packed brown sugar
1/2 cup white wine
2 tablespoons finely chopped fresh cilantro

Combine the apricots, olives, olive oil, vinegar, oregano, capers, garlic, bay leaves, salt and pepper in a bowl. Arrange the chicken in a 9×13-inch baking dish. Pour the marinade over the chicken. Sprinkle with the brown sugar. Pour the wine over the top. Marinate, covered, in the refrigerator for 8 to 12 hours.

Bring to room temperature. Bake, uncovered, at 350 degrees for 40 minutes or until cooked through, basting frequently with the pan juices. (Do not overcook. Check the chicken frequently for doneness after 30 minutes of baking.)

Remove the chicken to a serving platter. Arrange the apricots, olives and capers around the chicken. Remove and discard the bay leaves. Pour the pan juices over the chicken. Sprinkle with the cilantro. Serve hot or at room temperature with Parmesan couscous, coarsely chopped Roma tomatoes and minced fresh basil.
Yield: 6 servings.

For my first wedding anniversary, I had planned an intimate Italian dinner with my husband as a surprise. I had secretly washed two place settings of our china and crystal, purchased the necessary ingredients, and left work early to prepare. I raced home, began cooking, and set the table. To my surprise, my husband shows up! He had picked up steaks and potatoes to prepare a supper for me. After only one year of marriage, we were already thinking alike! We enjoyed the Italian dinner that night and the steaks the next night. Over both dinners, we laughed about surprising each other for our first anniversary.
Julie Ann Walker

Pecan-Stuffed Chicken Breasts

1 tablespoon butter
$^1/_2$ cup finely chopped celery
$^1/_2$ cup finely chopped carrot
$^1/_2$ cup finely chopped onion
2 tablespoons poultry seasoning
1 tablespoon celery salt
5 cups coarse bread crumbs
2 cups chopped pecans
1 cup rich chicken stock
2 eggs
Salt and pepper to taste
6 boneless chicken breasts, trimmed
$^1/_3$ cup butter, melted
2 teaspoons fresh lemon juice

Melt 1 tablespoon butter in a hot skillet. Add the celery, carrot, onion, poultry seasoning and celery salt. Sauté until the onion is tender. Remove to a bowl. Stir in the bread crumbs, pecans, chicken stock and eggs. Season with salt and pepper. Spoon into a greased baking dish. Bake at 350 degrees for about 45 minutes or until the stuffing is somewhat dry. Cool completely.

Place the chicken skin side down on plastic wrap. Combine $^1/_3$ cup melted butter and the lemon juice in a bowl. Brush over the chicken to coat lightly. Cover with another sheet of plastic wrap. Pound the chicken gently with the side of a meat mallet until of a uniform thickness. Remove the top layer of plastic wrap. Place a generous portion of the pecan stuffing on each piece of chicken. Wrap the chicken around the stuffing to enclose completely. Place in a baking dish. Brush the chicken with the lemon-butter mixture. Bake at 350 degrees for 45 minutes or until the chicken is cooked through. *Yield: 6 to 8 servings.*

Raffi's, a popular Evansville restaurant, was founded in 1989 by Raffi Manna. Diners at this upscale local hot spot can always count on the cheerful greetings and handshakes of its owner, who, once upon a time, was not a chef but an engineer.

While studying for his engineering degree, Raffi worked first as a dishwasher and busboy, observing and learning about the restaurant business. Finding himself smitten by the field, he gradually worked his way up to manager and then executive chef of Ciraco's in Nashville. By the time he completed his degree, Raffi had changed professional directions, leaving engineering behind for his new goal of owning and running a restaurant.

(continued on next page)

140

Chef Graham's Chicken

Raffi's Restaurant

2 (4-ounce) chicken breasts
Flour for dredging
1 tablespoon vegetable oil
3 to 4 tablespoons butter
1 green apple, chopped
2 ounces dried cranberries
1 tablespoon chopped fresh sage

Dredge the chicken in flour. Heat the oil in a skillet. Add the chicken. Brown on both sides until cooked through; set aside.

Melt the butter in a saucepan. Add the apple, cranberries and sage. Cook for 2 to 3 minutes. Pour over the chicken. *Yield: 2 servings.*

Queen of England

Raffi's Restaurant

2 (4-ounce) chicken breasts
Flour for dredging
1 tablespoon vegetable oil
1 cup honey
$1/2$ cup red grape halves
$1/4$ cup chopped walnuts

Dredge the chicken in flour. Heat the oil in an ovenproof skillet. Add the chicken. Cook on both sides until brown. Remove the skillet to the oven. Bake at 325 degrees for 30 to 45 minutes or until the chicken is cooked through, checking at 30 minutes.

Cook the honey, grapes and walnuts in a saucepan until warm. Pour over the chicken. *Yield: 2 servings.*

Enchiladas Verdes con Pollo

4 cups coarsely shredded cooked chicken or turkey
2 cups (8 ounces) shredded Monterey Jack or
Pepper Jack cheese
1 (7-ounce) can diced green chiles
1 1/2 teaspoons oregano
Salt to taste
Vegetable oil for frying
12 (6-inch) corn tortillas
4 to 6 ounces prepared tomatillo sauce
1 cup (4 ounces) shredded Monterey Jack or
Pepper Jack cheese
1 to 1 1/2 cups sour cream
1/2 cup chopped fresh cilantro
1 or 2 tomatillos, husked, thinly sliced, or 1 lime, sliced

Combine the chicken, 2 cups cheese, green chiles and oregano in a large bowl. Season with salt; set aside.

Pour the oil into a large skillet to a 1/4-inch depth. Heat over medium-high heat until hot. Add the tortillas 1 at a time to the hot oil. Cook for about 10 seconds or just until limp and slightly blistered, turning once. Add more oil to the skillet as needed. Drain on paper towels.

Spoon 1/2 cup of the chicken mixture down the center of each warm tortilla. Roll the tortilla around the filling. Place seam side down in a 10×15-inch baking pan. Cover the pan with foil. (May prepare the enchiladas a day ahead to this point and refrigerate. Add 10 minutes to the baking time.) Bake, covered, at 350 degrees for 35 minutes. Uncover and top with the tomatillo sauce and 1 cup cheese. Bake, uncovered, for about 10 minutes or until the cheese melts. Serve the enchiladas topped with sour cream, cilantro and sliced tomatillos.
Yield: 6 servings.

With his supportive wife, Renee, by his side, Raffi fulfilled his dream. Raffi's is known for its unique menu that features innovative steak, pasta, seafood, lamb, chicken, and duck entrées—and for its unparalleled service. Though elegant and highly professional, the restaurant, like its owner, is as comfortable as a best friend and is a delightful setting for special occasions and everyday celebrations.

Chicken Casserole Divan

It's easier than you think to make your own bread crumbs! Just place slices of bread into a blender and pulse. Add bread until you have enough crumbs for your recipe. Experiment with different types of bread: white, wheat, 7-grain, French, Italian. This is a great way to use bread that has dried out a bit.

142

4 whole chicken breasts
4 cups chopped broccoli, steamed (1 pound)
1 (10-ounce) can cream of mushroom soup
$^3/_4$ cup sour cream
$^1/_2$ cup mayonnaise
$^1/_4$ cup white wine
2 cups (8 ounces) shredded Cheddar cheese
$^3/_4$ to 1 cup bread crumbs
2 tablespoons butter, melted

Place the chicken in a microwave-safe bowl. Add enough water to cover the chicken. Microwave on High for 15 to 20 minutes or until the chicken is cooked through; cool. Remove the chicken from the bone, discarding the skin and bones. Cut the chicken into bite-size pieces.

Spoon the broccoli into a 9×13-inch baking dish. Top with the chicken. Combine the soup, sour cream, mayonnaise and wine in a bowl. Pour over the chicken. Sprinkle with the cheese and bread crumbs. Drizzle the butter over the top. Bake at 350 degrees for 30 to 40 minutes. *Yield: 8 servings.*

NOTE: MAY BE PREPARED A DAY AHEAD, COVERED AND REFRIGERATED. DO NOT ADD THE BREAD CRUMB AND BUTTER TOPPING UNTIL JUST BEFORE BAKING.

Chicken Croissants

4 or 5 chicken breasts, cooked, shredded
1 (8-ounce) can mushrooms, drained, coarsely chopped
1 (8-ounce) package chive and onion cream cheese, softened

6 tablespoons margarine, melted
Salt and pepper to taste
2 (8-count) cans crescent rolls
Italian-style bread crumbs

Combine the chicken, mushrooms, cream cheese, margarine, salt and pepper in a bowl and mix well. Drop the chicken mixture into eight ³/₄-cup mounds on a baking sheet. Chill, covered, for 8 to 12 hours or freeze just until firm.

Separate the crescent roll dough into 8 rectangles, pressing the perforations together to seal. Place 1 mound of the chicken mixture on each rectangle. Wrap the crescent roll dough around the mound, forming a ball. Roll in bread crumbs and place on a baking sheet. Bake at 350 degrees for 25 minutes or until golden brown. *Yield: 8 servings.*

NOTE: MAY DOUBLE THE AMOUNT OF CREAM CHEESE IF A CREAMIER TEXTURE IS DESIRED. MAY MAKE THE CHICKEN MIXTURE AHEAD AND STORE THE MOUNDS IN THE FREEZER. THAW BEFORE USING.

143

Chicken and Artichoke Casserole

1 cup (2 sticks) butter
¹/₂ cup flour
3¹/₂ cups milk
¹/₂ teaspoon MSG
¹/₂ teaspoon garlic powder
¹/₂ teaspoon cayenne pepper
1 cup (4 ounces) shredded Cheddar cheese

3 ounces Gruyère cheese, shredded
5 poached chicken breasts, coarsely chopped
1 pound fresh mushrooms, sliced
2 (14-ounce) cans quartered artichoke hearts, drained
¹/₂ to 1 (3-ounce) can French-fried onions

Melt the butter in a saucepan over medium heat. Add the flour gradually, stirring until smooth. Blend in the milk gradually. Stir in the MSG, garlic powder and cayenne pepper. Add the Cheddar cheese and Gruyère cheese. Cook until thickened, stirring constantly. Stir in the chicken, mushrooms and artichoke hearts. Pour into a 9×13-inch baking dish. Top with a desired amount of French-fried onions. Bake at 350 degrees for 45 minutes. *Yield: 8 servings.*

NOTE: THIS DISH TASTES BEST WHEN PREPARED AND COOKED THE DAY BEFORE AND THEN REHEATED BEFORE SERVING.

Turkey Tetrazzini

2¹/₂ cups broken spaghetti
1¹/₂ quarts boiling water
¹/₄ cup (¹/₂ stick) butter
3 tablespoons chopped onion
2¹/₂ to 3 cups cubed cooked turkey
1 (12-ounce) can evaporated milk
1 (10-ounce) can cream of chicken soup
1 (7-ounce) jar mushrooms
1 (4-ounce) jar chopped pimentos, drained
¹/₂ cup (2 ounces) cubed sharp Cheddar cheese
1 to 2 tablespoons dry sherry
¹/₂ teaspoon salt
¹/₂ teaspoon celery seeds
¹/₂ teaspoon marjoram
¹/₄ teaspoon nutmeg
Salt and pepper to taste
¹/₂ cup (2 ounces) grated Parmesan or Romano cheese

Cook the spaghetti in the water until tender. Drain and rinse; set aside.

Melt the butter in a skillet. Add the onion. Cook until translucent. Stir in the turkey, evaporated milk, soup, mushrooms, pimentos, Cheddar cheese, sherry, salt, celery seeds, marjoram and nutmeg. Cook until the cheese melts. Season with salt and pepper.

Place the spaghetti in a buttered 8×11-inch baking dish. Pour the chicken mixture over the top. Sprinkle with the Parmesan cheese. Bake at 325 degrees for 45 minutes. *Yield: 8 servings.*

NOTE: MAY BE PREPARED AHEAD, COVERED AND REFRIGERATED OR FROZEN.

Meg Dettwiler and I were friends for 25 years, and we were unable to say "no" to entertaining for our volunteer organizations. Meg died in August 1999, just before she planned to help me with another event. Together we created what became known as "Our Famous Tetrazzini." This was our standard fare to serve for organizations, family, and friends. Our most ambitious event was a winter museum dinner for 120 people. Between turkeys in the oven and on the stove, my windows were dripping wet with condensation and it was about 90+ degrees in my kitchen!

Enjoy this recipe from Meg and me.

Jean Brubeck

144

Turkey Burgers with a Kick

1 pound ground turkey breast
½ cup (2 ounces) shredded
 Monterey Jack cheese
2 scallions, minced
1 tablespoon soy sauce

1 tablespoon ketchup
¼ teaspoon garlic powder
¼ teaspoon freshly ground pepper
4 hamburger buns, toasted

Combine the turkey breast, cheese, scallions, soy sauce, ketchup, garlic powder and pepper in a bowl. Shape into 4 patties. Grill or broil for 6 to 8 minutes on each side or until cooked through. Serve on the buns with your favorite toppings. *Yield: 4 servings.*

Paella

⅓ cup olive oil
2 boneless skinless chicken breasts
3 links Italian sausage, cut into pieces
1 cup chopped onion
2 garlic cloves, chopped
2 (14-ounce) cans chicken broth
2½ teaspoons salt
1 teaspoon white pepper

1 teaspoon saffron
½ teaspoon paprika
2 cups uncooked rice
1 (16-ounce) can diced tomatoes
1½ pounds deveined peeled fresh shrimp
1 (10-ounce) package frozen peas, thawed
1 (7-ounce) can artichoke hearts, drained

Heat the olive oil in a large pan. Add the chicken and sausage. Sauté until golden brown. Remove and set aside.

   Add the onion and garlic to the oil in the pan. Sauté until golden brown. Add the chicken broth, salt, white pepper, saffron and paprika. Bring to a boil. Stir in the rice. Cook, covered, until about half the liquid is absorbed. Add the tomatoes, chicken, sausage and shrimp. Simmer, covered, for about 45 minutes or until the rice is almost dry. Add the peas and artichoke hearts and toss. Serve heaped in a large casserole. *Yield: 6 servings.*

Baking Fish

Fish that bake well include bass, catfish, flounder, grouper, halibut, mahimahi, orange roughy, pompano, red snapper, shark, sole, and trout. The basic guide to baking fish: bake in a moderate oven (350 degrees) for 10 minutes per inch of thickness.

Basil Baked Fish

¹/₂ cup white wine or water	Juice and zest of 1 lemon or lime
1 tablespoon butter	Salt and pepper to taste
1 cup basil leaves	¹/₂ teaspoon onion powder
4 thin fish fillets (such as tilapia, flounder, red snapper or trout)	2 tablespoons plain fine bread crumbs
	Paprika to taste

Pour the wine into a 2-cup glass measuring cup. Add the butter. Microwave on High for about 1 minute or until the butter begins to melt; set aside.

Spread the basil leaves over the bottom of a 9×13-inch baking dish. Place the fish fillets over the basil. Stir the lemon juice and lemon zest into the wine mixture. Pour over the fish. Season the fish with salt and pepper. Sprinkle with the onion powder, bread crumbs and paprika. Bake, covered, at 450 degrees in the lower third of the oven for 12 minutes. Uncover the dish. Continue baking for 2 to 3 minutes or until the fish flakes easily. *Yield: 4 servings.*

Fiddlers

Fiddlers are small, whole, cornmeal-breaded and fried young catfish. Go to page 55 for more on these Evansville treats!

1 cup milk	¹/₂ cup fine white cornmeal
1 egg	4 fiddlers, fins removed
¹/₂ cup cracker meal or crushed crackers	Vegetable oil for frying

Combine the milk and egg in a shallow dish. Combine the cracker meal and cornmeal in another shallow dish. Dip the fiddlers in the milk mixture and then in the meal mixture. Pour the oil into a large skillet to a 1-inch depth and heat until hot. Add the fiddlers. Fry for about 20 minutes or until the fish are golden brown and flake easily. *Yield: 4 servings.*

Asian Roasted Monkfish with Sesame Spinach

Rolling Hills Country Club, Executive Chef Michael Dell, C.E.C.

Teriyaki Marinade

¹/₂ cup soy sauce	1 teaspoon sesame oil
¹/₂ cup teriyaki sauce	14 ounces monkfish fillet
¹/₄ cup pineapple juice	Salt and pepper to taste
2 teaspoons minced fresh gingerroot	

Sauce

¹/₄ cup butter	1 tablespoon soy sauce
¹/₄ cup sesame seeds	1 tablespoon fresh lemon juice
1 teaspoon minced fresh gingerroot	1 teaspoon cornstarch
1 teaspoon minced garlic	¹/₂ cup sliced scallions
1 cup chicken stock	

Sesame Spinach

¹/₄ cup sesame oil	8 ounces fresh baby spinach
¹/₄ cup sesame seeds	

For the teriyaki marinade, combine the soy sauce, teriyaki sauce, pineapple juice, gingerroot and sesame oil in a bowl. Place the monkfish in the marinade. Marinate at room temperature for 1 hour.

Remove the monkfish from the marinade; discard the marinade. Season the fish with salt and pepper. Sear all sides of the fish in an ovenproof sauté pan. Place the pan in a 350-degree oven. Bake for 15 minutes or until the fish flakes easily. Remove from the oven; set aside and keep warm.

For the sauce, melt the butter in a sauté pan. Add the sesame seeds. Toast until golden brown. Stir in the gingerroot and garlic. Combine the chicken stock, soy sauce, lemon juice and cornstarch in a bowl, stirring until smooth. Add to the sesame seed mixture. Bring to a simmer. Cook until thickened. Stir in the scallions; set aside and keep warm.

For the sesame spinach, heat the sesame oil in a sauté pan. Add the sesame seeds to the hot oil. When the sesame seeds begin to brown, add the spinach. Cook just until the spinach is wilted. Remove the spinach to a serving plate, forming a bed. Slice the monkfish into medallions and place over the bed of spinach.

Spoon the sauce over the fish. Serve immediately. *Yield: 2 servings.*

Maple Mustard Salmon

1 tablespoon olive oil
3/4 cup yellow mustard seeds
1/4 cup Dijon mustard
1/4 cup maple syrup
2 teaspoons balsamic vinegar
1/2 teaspoon coarse salt
1/4 teaspoon freshly ground pepper
4 (6- to 8-ounce) salmon fillets

Heat the olive oil in a skillet over medium-low heat. Add the mustard seeds and stir to coat, adding more oil if needed. Cook, covered, until the seeds begin to pop. Remove from the heat, but keep the pan covered until the popping stops; set aside.

Whisk the Dijon mustard, maple syrup, vinegar, salt and pepper together in a shallow dish. Taste and adjust the seasonings. Stir in the mustard seeds. Place the salmon fillets in the mustard marinade, turning to coat. Marinate, covered, in the refrigerator for 30 minutes. Remove from the refrigerator and let stand at room temperature for 10 minutes.

Remove the salmon from the marinade to a foil-lined baking sheet; reserve the marinade. Spoon the mustard seeds from the marinade over the salmon. Cover the fillets with a piece of foil or parchment paper. Bake at 450 degrees for 5 minutes. Uncover the salmon. Bake for 5 minutes longer or until the fish flakes easily, checking every minute after the first 10 minutes of baking time. Serve with wild rice pilaf or fresh baby greens drizzled with lemon juice. *Yield: 4 servings.*

Orange Bourbon Salmon

¹/₄ cup bourbon
¹/₄ cup fresh orange juice
¹/₄ cup low-sodium soy sauce
¹/₄ cup packed brown sugar
3 tablespoons chopped fresh chives

¹/₄ cup chopped green onions
2 tablespoons fresh lemon juice
2 teaspoons chopped garlic
4 (6-ounce) salmon fillets

Combine the bourbon, orange juice, soy sauce, brown sugar, chives, green onions, lemon juice and garlic in a large sealable plastic bag. Add the salmon fillets; seal the bag. Marinate in the refrigerator for at least 2 hours, turning the bag occasionally.

Remove the salmon from the marinade; reserve the marinade. Grill over medium coals for about 6 minutes on each side or until the fish flakes easily, basting with the reserved marinade. Discard any remaining marinade. *Yield: 4 servings.*

Simple Salmon

2 fresh salmon fillets of equal size
Olive oil to taste
Coarse salt and cracked pepper to taste

Fresh dill weed sprigs to taste
Whole chives to taste
1 lemon, sliced

Place 1 salmon fillet skin side down on a sheet of foil. Drizzle with olive oil and lightly season with salt and pepper. Top with dill weed, chives and the lemon slices. Place the second fillet skin side up over the lemon. Wrap the fish with more foil. Marinate in the refrigerator for 3 hours.

Bake the foil-wrapped fish at 350 degrees, or grill, for about 20 minutes or until the fish flakes easily. Serve with Tartar Sauce (at right). *Yield: 2 servings.*

Tartar Sauce

¹/₂ cup mayonnaise

1 tablespoon chopped shallot

1 dill pickle, chopped

Combine the mayonnaise, shallot and pickle in a bowl. Chill, covered, before serving.

Yield: 4 servings

Shrimp with Feta

2 cups rice	¹⁄₄ cup chopped fresh parsley
2 teaspoons olive oil	1 garlic clove, crushed
¹⁄₄ cup coarsely chopped Vidalia or	¹⁄₂ teaspoon salt
other sweet onion	¹⁄₂ teaspoon basil
1¹⁄₂ pounds deveined peeled large shrimp	¹⁄₂ teaspoon oregano
2 (14-ounce) cans no-salt-added	¹⁄₄ teaspoon dill weed
diced tomatoes	¹⁄₄ teaspoon crushed red pepper
¹⁄₃ cup dry white wine	4 ounces feta cheese, crumbled

Cook the rice according to the package directions.

Heat the olive oil in a nonstick skillet coated with nonstick cooking spray over medium-high heat. Add the onion. Sauté for 4 minutes. Stir in the shrimp, tomatoes, wine, parsley, garlic, salt, basil, oregano, dill weed and crushed red pepper. Cook for 3 minutes or until the shrimp turn pink. Remove from the heat. Sprinkle with the cheese. Serve over the rice. *Yield: 4 to 6 servings.*

Lobster Newburg

¹⁄₄ cup (¹⁄₂ stick) butter or margarine	1 pint heavy cream
2 tablespoons flour	2 egg yolks, beaten
1 teaspoon salt	12 ounces cooked lobster meat, cut into
¹⁄₄ teaspoon paprika	¹⁄₂-inch pieces
Dash of cayenne pepper	2 tablespoons sherry or vermouth

Melt the butter in a large heavy saucepan. Blend in the flour, salt, paprika and cayenne pepper. Add the cream. Cook until thickened and creamy, stirring constantly. Stir a little of the hot cream sauce into the egg yolks in a bowl. Add the egg yolk mixture to the remaining sauce in the saucepan, stirring constantly. Add the lobster and heat through. Remove from the heat. Stir in the sherry gradually. Serve immediately over rice or toast points. *Yield: 4 servings.*

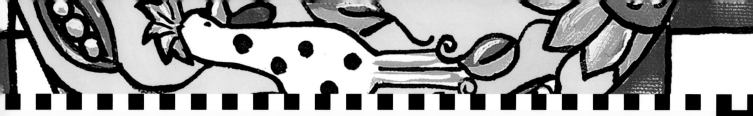

Spinach Lasagna

8 ounces sliced fresh mushrooms
1 medium carrot, chopped
$^1/_2$ cup chopped onion
4 garlic cloves, finely chopped
2 tablespoons butter
3 cups heavy cream
1 teaspoon salt
1 teaspoon nutmeg
$^1/_2$ teaspoon pepper
2 teaspoons cornstarch (optional)
4 cups (16 ounces) shredded mozzarella cheese
1 cup (4 ounces) grated Parmesan cheese
1 pound lasagna noodles, cooked, drained
2 (10-ounce) packages frozen chopped spinach, thawed, well drained

Sauté the mushrooms, carrot, onion and garlic in the butter in a saucepan until tender. Stir in the cream, salt, nutmeg and pepper. Bring to a boil. Reduce the heat to low. Simmer for 30 minutes or until thickened, stirring frequently. (If the vegetable sauce is too thin, add the cornstarch.) Combine the mozzarella cheese and Parmesan cheese in a bowl.

Layer 3 to 4 noodles, $^1/_2$ of the spinach, $^1/_2$ of the vegetable sauce and $^1/_3$ of the cheese in a greased 9×13-inch baking pan. Continue layering with $^1/_2$ of the remaining noodles, the remaining spinach, remaining vegetable sauce and $^1/_2$ of the remaining cheese. Top with the remaining noodles and cheese.

Bake, covered, at 375 degrees for 40 minutes or until bubbly. Let stand for 15 minutes before serving. *Yield: 8 to 10 servings.*

NOTE: MAY BE PREPARED AHEAD OF TIME AND FROZEN. ASSEMBLE THE UNBAKED LASAGNA AS DIRECTED ABOVE, OMITTING THE LAST LAYER OF CHEESE. COVER TIGHTLY WITH HEAVY-DUTY FOIL AND FREEZE. THAW SLOWLY IN THE REFRIGERATOR FOR 2 DAYS. ADD THE CHEESE TOPPING. BAKE AS DIRECTED ABOVE.

Gourmet Baked Pasta

2 cups finely chopped onions
2 garlic cloves, minced
1 teaspoon basil, crumbled
1 teaspoon oregano, crumbled
$1/2$ teaspoon crushed red pepper
2 tablespoons olive oil
1 pound fresh shiitake mushrooms, stemmed, sliced
6 tablespoons unsalted butter
6 tablespoons flour
4 cups milk (skim or 2%)
2 (28-ounce) cans whole Italian tomatoes, well drained, chopped

4 ounces sliced prosciutto, cut into strips
8 ounces fontina cheese, shredded
8 ounces Gorgonzola cheese, crumbled
$1^{1}/2$ cups (6 ounces) freshly grated Parmesan cheese
$2/3$ cup minced fresh parsley
1 pound penne or farfalle
Salt and black pepper to taste
$1/4$ cup (1 ounce) freshly grated Parmesan cheese
2 tablespoons unsalted butter, cut into small pieces

Cook the onions, garlic, basil, oregano and crushed red pepper in the olive oil in a large skillet over low heat until the onion is tender. Add the mushrooms. Cook over medium heat for 10 minutes or until the mushrooms are tender. Remove from the heat; set aside.

Melt 6 tablespoons butter in a saucepan over medium heat. Add the flour. Cook for 3 minutes, whisking constantly. Whisk in the milk gradually. Cook until thickened, whisking constantly. Add the white sauce, tomatoes, prosciutto, fontina cheese, Gorgonzola cheese, $1^{1}/2$ cups Parmesan cheese and the parsley to the mushroom mixture.

Cook the penne in a pot of boiling salted water for 5 minutes; drain well. (The pasta will not be tender.) Add the penne to the mushroom mixture. Season with salt and black pepper and toss well.

Spoon into a buttered 4-quart baking dish. Sprinkle with $1/4$ cup Parmesan cheese. Dot with 2 tablespoons butter. Bake at 450 degrees for 25 to 30 minutes or until the top is golden brown and the pasta is tender. *Yield: 8 servings.*

Greek Lemon Chicken Pasta

Lemon Marinade

1 cup chablis	1 teaspoon freshly ground pepper
1/4 cup olive oil	3 garlic cloves, crushed
1/4 cup fresh lemon juice	4 or 5 boneless skinless large whole
1 teaspoon grated lemon zest	chicken breasts
1 teaspoon salt	

Sauce

2 tablespoons butter	Grated zest of 1 lemon
2 tablespoons flour	1 teaspoon fresh lemon juice
1/2 teaspoon salt	1/4 cup minced fresh parsley
2 teaspoons Dijon mustard	1 teaspoon dill weed, or 1 tablespoon
1 cup milk	fresh chopped dill weed
2 egg yolks	1 cup sour cream

Pasta

1/4 cup (1/2 stick) butter, melted	12 ounces warm angel hair pasta, cooked al dente
3/4 cup (3 ounces) crumbled feta cheese	3/4 cup (3 ounces) shredded fontina cheese

For the lemon marinade, combine the chablis, olive oil, lemon juice, lemon zest, salt, pepper and garlic in a bowl. Pound the chicken lightly. Place in a shallow dish or sealable plastic bag. Pour the marinade over the chicken. Marinate, covered, in the refrigerator for up to 12 hours. Remove the chicken and marinade to a saucepan. Add enough water to cover the chicken. Poach for 30 minutes or until the chicken is tender and cooked through. Discard the marinade. Cut the chicken into bite-size pieces; set aside.

For the sauce, melt the butter in a saucepan. Blend in the flour and salt to make a roux. Stir in the Dijon mustard. Add the milk gradually, stirring constantly. Cook until thick and smooth, stirring constantly. Combine the egg yolks, lemon zest and lemon juice in a small bowl. Whisk a small amount of the sauce into the egg mixture. Whisk the egg mixture into the remaining sauce. Bring to a simmer. Remove from the heat. Add the parsley and dill weed. When the parsley wilts, stir in the sour cream.

For the pasta, add the butter, 3/4 cup of the sauce and the feta cheese to the warm pasta and mix well. Place in a greased 9×13-inch baking dish. Top with the chicken pieces, remaining sauce and fontina cheese. Bake, covered, at 350 degrees for 50 minutes. Uncover the baking dish. Continue baking for 10 minutes. *Yield: 10 servings.*

Roasted Garlic Tomato Sauce with Penne Pasta

Here's an idea for leftover French bread. Take a leftover loaf and slice to, but not through, the bottom crust. Spread the cut pieces with a mixture of melted butter, garlic powder, and dried parsley. Wrap in foil and freeze. To use, heat the foil-wrapped loaf in the oven.

154

1 head garlic
2 tablespoons olive oil
$^1/_4$ cup olive oil
1 (28-ounce) can whole Italian plum tomatoes
$^1/_2$ teaspoon coarse salt
Freshly ground pepper to taste
$^1/_2$ cup fresh basil leaves, coarsely chopped or torn
1 pound penne, cooked, drained
Freshly grated Parmesan cheese

Remove and discard all but 1 layer of the outer papery peel from the head of garlic. Place on a square of foil. Drizzle with 2 tablespoons olive oil. Fold the foil up around the garlic to seal. Place in a shallow baking dish. Bake at 350 degrees for about 45 minutes; cool completely. Remove individual roasted cloves by pinching and squeezing at the bottom. Reserve 4 or 5 roasted cloves. (Refrigerate the remaining roasted cloves, covered, for up to 1 week.)

Heat $^1/_4$ cup olive oil in a skillet over medium heat. Add the undrained tomatoes, salt and pepper, breaking up the tomatoes with the side of a wooden spoon. Mash the reserved garlic. Add to the tomatoes. Bring to a boil. Reduce the heat to low. Simmer for 20 to 30 minutes or until the sauce thickens, stirring occasionally. Remove from the heat. Stir in the basil. Toss the sauce with the penne. Top with the cheese. *Yield: 4 servings.*

Old World Linguini with Clams

The Pasta Grill

1 cup clam juice
$^1/_2$ cup olive oil
4 teaspoons minced garlic
4 teaspoons basil
4 teaspoons butter
4 pinches of paprika
4 pinches of white pepper
1 pound chopped clams
2$^1/_4$ pounds cooked linguini
4 pinches of freshly grated Parmigiano-Reggiano cheese
$^1/_2$ cup white wine

Combine the clam juice, olive oil, garlic, basil, butter, paprika and white pepper in a pot. Cook until heated through. Add the clams. Simmer for 1 minute. Do not overcook. Add the linguini and cheese. Add the wine and stir to deglaze the pan. Mix well and heat for about 15 seconds. Serve immediately. *Yield: 6 servings.*

How much is enough? Here's a tip for measuring pasta: Grab a handful of spaghetti—an 8-ounce portion measures 2 inches in diameter. Smaller-size pasta may be measured in a measuring cup.

Back to Basics

A River Runs Through Us

Proud of its heritage as a river city, Evansville celebrates the mighty Ohio with annual festivals, outdoor concerts, and activities on the newly renovated Dress Plaza. A walk along the picturesque esplanade reveals historic neighborhoods, cultural attractions, and thriving corporations both large and small. Barges bearing cargoes of coal and other goods travel up and down the Ohio, carrying with them the stories of ports of call from the deep south to the north. Evansville's most well-known river story is most likely that of the infamous flood of 1937, when the river flooded for 42 days, leaving more than 400 city blocks under water.

Beautifully situated on the river is the Evansville Museum of Arts, History and Science, which houses collections dating from the 16th century to the present, a planetarium, and a replica of Evansville's early main street. Next door, the "Pagoda," built in 1912, once served as a Japanese-style park venue for Sunday afternoon concerts and is now the charming home of the Evansville Convention and Visitors Bureau. Just steps away from the Ohio River lies Evansville's historic district, featuring turn-of-the-century homes and brick-lined streets reminiscent of an era when, *once upon a time*, Victorian parlors were the settings for teas and society gatherings.

Standing tall along the bend in the river rises the city's Four Freedoms Monument, which was dedicated in 1976 in celebration of the country's bicentennial. The four commanding columns were constructed in 1882 to be the front pillars of a downtown railroad depot. Today, they represent four of our nation's most beloved freedoms: freedom of speech, freedom of religion, freedom from fear, and freedom from oppression. For some, it has become a place of solace and comfort in times of need.

Casino Aztar's *Spirit of Evansville* is permanently docked on the Ohio. The historic riverboat casino boasts several restaurants, a hotel, and often features live music. The entire riverfront virtually explodes with excitement for one week each summer during the annual Freedom Festival, an Independence Day celebration that attracts thousands. A perennial favorite, Thunder on the Ohio, features hydroplane races and air shows. Concerts, carnival rides, and ever-present food booths appeal to young and old alike.

From fine art to firework, festivities abound along the river. However, the riverfront is also a place for quiet contemplation and leisurely strolls. The river draws us to its banks for many reasons and is as much a part of Evansville as the streets that lead us there.

Comfort Food

Simple Seven-Layer Bean Dip

1 (9-ounce) can bean dip
3 or 4 avocados
1 tablespoon lemon juice
1 cup mayonnaise
8 ounces sour cream
1 envelope taco seasoning mix
8 ounces Cheddar cheese, shredded
1 large tomato, coarsely chopped
3 bunches green onions, coarsely chopped
1 (6-ounce) can black olives, drained, sliced
Tortilla chips

Spread the bean dip on a serving platter. Mash the avocados in a bowl. Stir in the lemon juice. Spread the avocados over the bean dip. Combine the mayonnaise, sour cream and taco seasoning mix in a bowl. Spread over the avocado layer. Top with layers of the cheese, tomato, green onions and olives. Refrigerate, covered, until chilled. Serve with tortilla chips. *Yield:* 10 *to* 12 *servings.*

Tuna Spread

3 (6-ounce) cans chunk light tuna, drained
8 ounces cream cheese, softened
2 tablespoons dried minced onion
2 tablespoons parsley flakes
2 tablespoons chili sauce
2 teaspoons hot sauce
Butter crackers

Combine the tuna, cream cheese, onion, parsley, chili sauce and hot sauce in a mixing bowl with an electric mixer. Spoon into a mold. Chill, covered, for 1 hour. Serve with crackers. *Yield:* 30 *servings.*

Grape Jelly Meatballs

2 pounds ground beef	1 (12-ounce) bottle chili sauce
1 egg, beaten	1 (10-ounce) jar grape jelly (1¼ cups)
Chopped onion to taste	Juice of 1 lemon (2 tablespoons)
Salt to taste	

Combine the ground beef, egg, onion and salt in a bowl. Roll into meatballs; set aside.

Combine the chili sauce, grape jelly and lemon juice in a saucepan. Bring to a simmer. Drop the meatballs into the simmering sauce. Simmer for 20 minutes or until cooked through. *Yield: 50 to 60 servings.*

NOTE: MAY BE PREPARED AHEAD OF TIME, COVERED AND CHILLED. BEFORE SERVING, BRING TO ROOM TEMPERATURE AND HEAT THROUGH.

Beef Stew

2 pounds stew beef, trimmed, cut into 1-inch cubes	5 carrots, cut into 1-inch pieces
¼ cup flour	3 potatoes, peeled, cut into 1-inch pieces
1 teaspoon salt	1 (28-ounce) can whole tomatoes
¼ teaspoon pepper	1 envelope onion soup mix
2 tablespoons vegetable oil	

Coat the beef cubes with the flour, salt and pepper. Place in a 3-quart baking dish. Add the oil and toss. Bake at 400 degrees for 30 minutes, stirring once. Reduce the oven temperature to 375 degrees.

Add the carrots, potatoes, tomatoes and onion soup mix. Bake, covered, for 2 hours or until the meat and vegetables are tender. *Yield: 6 servings.*

Sunday Favorite Brisket

1 (6- to 8-pound) beef brisket
¹/₂ to ³/₄ cup ketchup
¹/₄ cup low-sodium soy sauce
6 garlic cloves, minced
1 large onion, thinly sliced
1 bay leaf

Trim off and discard any excess fat from the brisket. Place fat side up in a shallow roasting pan. Combine the ketchup, soy sauce and garlic in a bowl. Using your hands, coat the brisket thoroughly on both sides with the ketchup mixture. Arrange the onion slices under and over the brisket. Add the bay leaf. Cover with foil. Roast at 350 degrees for 2 to 2¹/₂ hours or until cooked through. Let stand for 15 minutes. Reduce the oven temperature to 300 degrees.

Remove the brisket from the pan, reserving the juices in the pan. Slice into long thin pieces. Return the slices to the pan. Bake for 20 to 30 minutes. (Or, chill in the pan until serving time and reheat at 300 degrees until heated through.) Remove and discard the bay leaf. Serve with a robust red wine. *Yield: 8 to 10 servings.*

NOTE: BRISKET IS TRADITIONALLY SERVED WITH POTATO LATKES AT HANUKKAH. IT MAY ALSO BE SERVED WITH MASHED OR BOILED POTATOES AND A HEARTY VEGETABLE.

My favorite comfort food is roast beef with mashed potatoes. It warms your belly and fills you up. My mother always made this for my special birthday dinners. Even my mother-in-law knows that this is my absolute favorite meal—she made it for me the night I came home from the hospital with my newborn baby.
Erika Taylor

Meat Loaf

Glaze (optional)
¹/₄ cup ketchup
2 tablespoons brown sugar
2 teaspoons spicy brown mustard

Meat Loaf
2¹/₂ pounds ground beef
2 eggs
1 onion, chopped
¹/₂ cup bread crumbs
¹/₄ cup ketchup
¹/₄ cup milk
2 to 3 tablespoons Worcestershire sauce
3 slices bacon (optional)

For the glaze, combine the ketchup, brown sugar and spicy brown mustard in a bowl; set aside.

For the meat loaf, mix all the ingredients in a bowl. Press into a loaf pan. Top with the bacon if not using the glaze. Bake at 350 degrees for 1¹/₂ hours or until cooked through, spreading the glaze over the top of the loaf during the last 15 minutes of baking. *Yield: 8 servings.*

My husband is really paranoid about food going bad. He won't even drink milk one day past the expiration date on the carton! Once when making a meat loaf for our family, I discovered that I was running short on ketchup. After digging around, I found some green ketchup that we had recently purchased. Since it tastes the same, I figured there was no harm in adding it to the meat loaf and saving the red ketchup for the top. After a few bites, my husband suddenly looked more closely at the meat loaf and asked me if the meat was okay. He then indicated that his piece was green. After I explained, he finished the meat loaf. He still reminds me not to use the green ketchup when I make meat loaf!

Julie Ann Walker

162

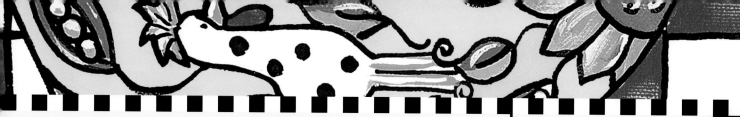

Best Italian Meatballs

1½ pounds extra-lean ground beef
2 eggs
¼ cup (1 ounce) freshly grated Parmesan cheese
2 tablespoons bread crumbs
1 tablespoon minced fresh parsley
1 tablespoon capers
1 garlic clove, minced, or 1 teaspoon garlic powder
Flour for dredging
1 tablespoon butter
1 tablespoon olive oil
⅓ cup white wine

Combine the ground beef, eggs, cheese, bread crumbs, parsley, capers and garlic in a bowl and mix well. Shape into 1-inch meatballs. Place the flour in a shallow bowl. Dredge the meatballs in the flour.

Heat the butter and olive oil in a large skillet. Add the meatballs. Sauté until cooked through. Remove from the skillet; set aside. Stir the wine into the skillet. Cook until somewhat reduced. Return the meatballs to the skillet. Cook until heated through. Serve with pasta and marinara sauce. *Yield: 6 servings.*

I grew up watching my mother make these meatballs. Even today, one of my favorite things to do is sit at the kitchen counter and watch my mother cook. When I was younger, it seemed like magic! Homemade breads, pastas, the world's best pizza...she could transform simple ingredients into anything! She is undoubtedly one of the most talented cooks I've ever had the pleasure of knowing and always takes the time to make special dishes for her family and friends. Now, I have two young sons who share my love for eating...and cooking! They sit at the kitchen counter, helping their "Mimi" mix flour and water, crack eggs, or carefully stir a simmering sauce. Whoever said "food isn't love" hasn't met my mother!
Francesca Brougham

163

Chicken Parmesan

2 eggs, lightly beaten
1 teaspoon salt
$\frac{1}{8}$ teaspoon pepper
1 cup fine dry unseasoned bread crumbs
6 whole chicken breasts, split, boned and skinned
$\frac{1}{2}$ cup vegetable oil
4 cups tomato sauce
1 tablespoon parsley
$\frac{1}{2}$ teaspoon basil
$\frac{1}{2}$ teaspoon oregano
$\frac{1}{8}$ teaspoon garlic powder
2 tablespoons butter
$\frac{1}{2}$ cup (2 ounces) grated Parmesan cheese
8 ounces mozzarella cheese, sliced or shredded

Combine the eggs, salt and pepper in a shallow dish. Place the bread crumbs in another shallow dish. Dip the chicken in the egg, then into the bread crumbs to coat.

Heat the oil in an electric skillet to 360 degrees. Add the chicken. Cook until brown on both sides. Remove the chicken to a 9×13-inch baking dish; set aside.

Combine the tomato sauce, parsley, basil, oregano and garlic powder in a saucepan. Bring to a boil. Reduce the heat to low. Simmer for 10 minutes. Stir in the butter. Pour over the chicken. Sprinkle with the Parmesan cheese.

Bake, covered, at 325 degrees for 30 minutes. Sprinkle with the mozzarella cheese. Bake, uncovered, for 10 minutes or until the chicken is cooked through. Serve with penne pasta.
Yield: 6 to 8 servings.

Lasagna

1 pound lean ground beef
2 tablespoons olive oil
1 large onion, chopped
2 or 3 garlic cloves, minced
2 tablespoons butter
1 (28-ounce) can diced tomatoes
1 (12-ounce) can tomato purée
1 (6-ounce) can tomato paste
¹/₄ cup red wine
1¹/₂ teaspoons sugar
1 teaspoon salt
1 teaspoon oregano
1 teaspoon basil

¹/₄ teaspoon black pepper
1 bay leaf
Crushed red pepper to taste
16 ounces ricotta cheese
1 (10-ounce) package frozen chopped
    spinach, thawed, well drained
2 eggs
1 tablespoon sugar
1 teaspoon freshly grated nutmeg
1 pound lasagna noodles, cooked,
    drained
16 ounces mozzarella cheese, shredded
1 cup (4 ounces) grated Parmesan cheese

Brown the ground beef in the olive oil in a skillet, stirring until crumbly; drain. Sauté the onion and garlic in the butter in a skillet. Combine the ground beef and onion mixture in a large pot. Add the tomatoes, tomato purée, tomato paste, wine, 1¹/₂ teaspoons sugar, salt, oregano, basil, black pepper, bay leaf and crushed red pepper. Bring to a boil. Reduce the heat to low. Simmer for 30 minutes.

Combine the ricotta cheese, spinach, eggs, 1 tablespoon sugar and nutmeg in a bowl and mix well.

Spread enough of the meat sauce over the bottom of a 9×13-inch baking dish to cover. Layer the noodles, ricotta mixture, remaining meat sauce, mozzarella cheese and Parmesan cheese ¹/₃ at a time in the baking dish. Bake at 350 degrees for 45 minutes or until bubbly. Let stand for 5 to 10 minutes before cutting. *Yield: 12 servings.*

Creamy Four-Cheese Macaroni

$^1/_3$ cup flour	3 ounces light Velveeta cheese
$2^2/_3$ cups 1% low-fat milk	6 cups cooked elbow macaroni
$^3/_4$ cup (3 ounces) shredded fontina or	(about 3 cups uncooked)
Swiss cheese	$^1/_4$ teaspoon salt
$^1/_2$ cup (2 ounces) freshly grated	$^1/_3$ cup crushed onion melba toast
Parmesan cheese	(about 12 slices)
$^1/_2$ cup (2 ounces) shredded extra-sharp	1 tablespoon margarine, softened
Cheddar cheese	

Place the flour in a saucepan. Add the milk gradually, whisking until blended. Cook over medium heat for 8 minutes or until thick, stirring constantly. Add the fontina cheese, Parmesan cheese, Cheddar cheese and Velveeta cheese. Cook for 3 minutes or until the cheese melts, stirring frequently. Remove from the heat. Stir in the macaroni and salt.

Spoon into a 2-quart baking dish coated with nonstick cooking spray. Combine the crushed melba toast and margarine in a small bowl and mix well. Sprinkle over the macaroni mixture. Bake at 375 degrees for 30 minutes or until bubbly. *Yield: 8 servings.*

Mama's Marinara

1 (28-ounce) can diced tomatoes, drained	2 tablespoons finely chopped fresh basil
1 (6-ounce) can tomato paste	2 teaspoons finely chopped fresh oregano
$^1/_2$ cup chopped onion	$^1/_4$ teaspoon salt
2 garlic cloves, minced	Pepper to taste
3 tablespoons olive oil	$^1/_4$ cup balsamic vinegar or dry red wine

Combine the tomatoes and tomato paste in a blender or food processor and process until smooth; set aside.

Sauté the onion and garlic in the olive oil in a skillet until the onion is tender. Add the tomato mixture, basil, oregano, salt and pepper. Simmer for 15 minutes. Add the vinegar. Continue simmering for 5 minutes. *Yield: 6 servings.*

NOTE: THIS SAUCE IS GREAT SERVED OVER ANGEL HAIR PASTA WITH FRESHLY GRATED PARMESAN CHEESE. USE ANY LEFTOVER SAUCE TO TOP CHICKEN PARMESAN.

Basic White Sauce (Béchamel)

2 tablespoons butter
2 tablespoons flour
1 cup milk
$\frac{1}{8}$ teaspoon nutmeg
Salt and pepper to taste

Melt the butter in a saucepan. Stir in the flour. Add the milk gradually, whisking constantly until smooth. Cook until thickened, stirring frequently. Add the nutmeg, salt and pepper. *Yield: 1 cup.*

VARIATIONS: OMIT THE NUTMEG AND STIR IN **2** TABLESPOONS SHERRY—GREAT WITH SEAFOOD. ADD $\frac{1}{4}$ CUP GRATED PARMESAN CHEESE—GREAT WITH PASTA AND VEGETABLES.

NOTE: FOR A VERY RICH ALFREDO-TYPE SAUCE, USE HALF MILK AND HALF HEAVY CREAM.

Basic Asian Marinade

$\frac{1}{2}$ cup soy sauce
$\frac{1}{2}$ cup beef broth or chicken broth
3 tablespoons sugar
1 teaspoon ginger
2 garlic cloves, minced
2 star anise, crushed
Crushed red pepper to taste (optional)
1 teaspoon sesame oil

Heat the soy sauce, beef broth, sugar, ginger, garlic, star anise and crushed red pepper in a saucepan until the sugar dissolves. Remove from the heat. Stir in the sesame oil. Pour over desired meat. Marinate, covered, in the refrigerator for 1 to 12 hours. Remove the meat from the marinade. Cook as desired, using the marinade as a basting sauce for grilled meats. Discard any remaining marinade. *Yield: 1 cup.*

All-American Apple Pie

7 or 8 tart apples, peeled, sliced
1¹/₂ tablespoons flour
³/₄ cup sugar
¹/₂ teaspoon cinnamon
¹/₂ teaspoon vanilla extract
¹/₈ teaspoon nutmeg
¹/₂ cup honey
¹/₃ cup flour
¹/₃ cup packed dark brown sugar
¹/₄ teaspoon cinnamon
¹/₈ teaspoon ginger
2 tablespoons butter
1 (2-crust) pie pastry, rolled out

Toss the apples with 1¹/₂ tablespoons flour in a large bowl. Add the sugar, ¹/₂ teaspoon cinnamon and vanilla and mix well. Stir in the honey. Let stand for 1 hour.

Combine ¹/₃ cup flour, the brown sugar, ¹/₄ teaspoon cinnamon and ginger in a small bowl. Cut in the butter until crumbly; set aside.

Fit 1 pastry into a 9-inch pie plate. Drain the apples, reserving the liquid. Reserve ¹/₄ cup of the crumb mixture. Layer the apples and remaining crumb mixture alternately in the pie plate until all of the ingredients are used. Drizzle with 5 tablespoons of the reserved apple liquid. Sprinkle with the reserved crumb mixture. Top with the remaining pastry, fluting the edge and cutting vents. Place the pie on a foil-lined baking sheet.

Bake at 450 degrees for 5 minutes. Reduce the oven temperature to 350 degrees. Bake for about 50 minutes or until golden brown. *Yield: 8 servings.*

Homemade Whipped Cream

Kids love this on hot chocolate!

1 cup whipping cream
2 tablespoons sugar
$^1/_2$ teaspoon vanilla extract

Combine the cream, sugar and vanilla in a chilled mixing bowl. Beat with chilled beaters at medium speed until soft peaks form.

To freeze leftover whipped cream, spoon the whipped cream into mounds on a waxed paper-lined baking sheet or plate. Vary the mound size depending on the desired portions. Freeze for 1 hour or until firm. Remove the mounds to a freezer bag or container. Freeze for up to 1 month. To serve, let the mounds stand for 5 minutes at room temperature before placing on top of a dessert or beverage. Yield: *2 cups.*

Evansville's Mesker Park Zoo and Botanical Gardens is the largest zoo in Indiana. Located on 70 acres of rolling, wooded terrain on the city's northwest side, it is open 365 days a year. Visitors can enjoy nearly 500 animals in natural habitat exhibits, including an interactive prairie dog exhibit and the beloved Donna, who, at 51, is the oldest living hippopotamus in captivity. For a nice change of pace, rent a paddleboat to cruise along the zoo's Lake Victoria, hop on board for a train ride, or explore the newly designed children's zoo. For those who enjoy a little literary trivia, the zoo's refurbished "Monkey Ship" (which no longer houses monkeys) is mentioned in the novel Lolita.

Happy
Endings

The Reitz Home- Evansville's Crown Jewel

Once upon a time, in a land far, far away, there lived a man who dreamed of a better life. So he traveled across the ocean to seek his fortune. After a long journey, he settled in a quiet river town and took a wife. It was there, along the peaceful riverbend, that the man realized his dream. The river town was green and lush, and the man was very wise, so he built a sawmill among the acres and acres of towering trees. The man worked very hard and after many years was rewarded for his efforts. From ocean to ocean, no one was more productive than he, and so he became known as the "Lumber Baron." Life was very good. The man and his wife were blessed many times over and, with their ten children, built a grand house just steps away from the river. In his beautiful home this man reflected upon his labors and his life and smiled, for he knew he would live out his days here by the magnificent river, happily ever after.

The man was John Augustus Reitz, a Prussian immigrant who settled in Evansville in the 1830s. The great success of his sawmill allowed him to build a unique home that has been meticulously preserved to this day. Open to the public, the Reitz Home Museum, as it is now known, is considered the "crown jewel" of Evansville's historic district. This Victorian home is a striking example of Second Empire architecture and features authentic period furniture, silk wall coverings, hand-painted ceilings, French chandeliers, marble fireplaces, and stained-glass windows.

Today, the Reitz Home is maintained for its cultural and educational value. Devoted volunteers help with everything from monthly cleaning to the "Living History" dramatizations, as well as implement fund-raisers such as the "Victorian Christmas" and interactive mystery dinners. The Reitz Home was placed on the National Register of Historic Places in 1973 and has recently been featured on Home and Garden Television (HGTV) along with the Rockefeller, Dupont, and Vanderbilt estates. It remains a beautiful tribute to our city's rich history and cultural heritage.

Desserts

Almond Pear Cake

1 cup flour
1 cup whole almonds (about 6 ounces)
2/3 cup sugar
2 eggs
1/4 cup (1/2 stick) unsalted butter, softened
2 tablespoons canola or corn oil
1 teaspoon baking powder
1 teaspoon vanilla extract
1/3 cup milk
3 tablespoons (about) sugar
3 large ripe pears (preferably Bartlett)
1/2 cup currant jam
1 tablespoon brandy or Cognac

Combine the flour, almonds and 2/3 cup sugar in a food processor and process until a coarse powder forms. Add the eggs, butter, canola oil, baking powder and vanilla and process just until mixed. Add the milk and process just until smooth. Pour into a generously buttered 10-inch springform pan.

Place 3 tablespoons sugar in a pie plate. Peel and cut the pears into halves; remove and discard the stems and cores. Rinse well in cold water. Roll the wet pears in the sugar. Push cut sides down into the cake batter, spacing them evenly around the pan. (The pears should be about half covered by the batter.) Place the pan on a baking sheet. Bake at 350 degrees for 40 minutes or until the cake is puffed and brown. Cool in the pan on a wire rack just until lukewarm.

Combine the jam and brandy in a bowl. Brush over the lukewarm cake. Remove the side of the pan. Cut the cake into 6 wedges so that each piece has a pear half. Serve warm or at room temperature with a dollop of whipped cream on the side if desired. *Yield: 6 servings.*

Banana Cake with Warm Caramel Icing

Cake

1 1/3 cups sugar	3/4 teaspoon salt
1/2 cup shortening	1 cup mashed bananas
2 eggs	1/2 cup buttermilk
2 cups cake flour	1 teaspoon vanilla extract
1 teaspoon baking powder	1/2 cup chopped walnuts
1 teaspoon baking soda	

Icing

2 cups sugar	2 tablespoons sugar
1/2 cup milk	1 teaspoon vanilla extract
1/3 cup light corn syrup	1 tablespoon margarine
Dash of salt	

For *the cake*, cream the sugar and shortening in a mixing bowl until light and fluffy. Add the eggs and beat until smooth. Sift the flour, baking powder, baking soda and salt together in a bowl. Add the flour mixture, bananas, buttermilk and vanilla to the creamed mixture. Beat for exactly 2 minutes. Fold in the walnuts. Pour into 2 greased and floured 9-inch round cake pans. Bake at 350 degrees for 25 to 30 minutes or until the layers test done. Cool in the pans for 10 minutes. Remove to wire racks to cool completely.

For *the icing*, combine 2 cups sugar, the milk, corn syrup and salt in a saucepan. Cook to 240 degrees on a candy thermometer, soft-ball stage; do not stir. Meanwhile, heat 2 tablespoons sugar in a small skillet until brown and caramelized, stirring constantly. Stir the caramelized sugar, vanilla and margarine into the milk mixture. Remove from the heat; cool. Beat the icing until it is thick enough to spread, adding milk if necessary to achieve the desired consistency. Spread between the layers and over the top and side of the cake. *Yield: 12 servings.*

NOTE: THE RIGHT ICING CONSISTENCY CAN BE DIFFICULT TO ACHIEVE. EVEN IF IT DOESN'T SPREAD WELL, THE CAKE WILL STILL TASTE GREAT!

Gourmet Carrot Cake with Cream Cheese Frosting

Victoria National Golf Club, Chef Douglas Rennie, C.E.C.

Cake

1 pound carrots, shredded	1 cup pecans, chopped
4¹/₄ cups flour	³/₄ cup raisins
2 cups sugar	5 eggs
1¹/₄ cups vegetable oil	4 teaspoons cinnamon
1 (8-ounce) can crushed pineapple	4 teaspoons vanilla extract
	3¹/₂ teaspoons baking soda
7 ounces shredded coconut	1 teaspoon salt

Frosting

12 ounces cream cheese, softened	6 cups confectioners' sugar
	1¹/₂ teaspoons vanilla extract
³/₄ cup (1¹/₂ sticks) margarine, softened	

For the cake, combine the carrots, flour, sugar, oil, undrained pineapple, coconut, pecans, raisins, eggs, cinnamon, vanilla, baking soda and salt in a mixing bowl. Mix with the paddle attachment of an electric mixer for about 5 minutes. Pour into two 9-inch round cake pans coated with nonstick cooking spray. Bake at 350 degrees for 45 to 55 minutes or until a wooden pick inserted in the center comes out clean. Cool in the pans for 1 hour. Remove from the pans to a baking sheet.

For the frosting, beat the cream cheese and margarine in a mixing bowl until well blended. Add the confectioners' sugar and vanilla. Beat until smooth and creamy. Spread between the layers and over the top and side of the cake. Yield: 12 *servings.*

On the outskirts of Evansville in the dramatic landscape of old coal mining property lies Victoria National Golf Club. The stripper pits that were created by the surface mining of coal resulted in a property so unique that world-renowned golf course architect Tom Fazio once described it as "Ballybunion in Ireland, only with water." This masterpiece sits on 417 acres and stretches from 5,200 to 7,369 yards. There are 118 tee boxes on 18 holes, so players of all skill levels can enjoy their walk in the park. All of this is topped off with a 12¹/₂-acre practice facility that also includes an outstanding short game area. You need to see it to believe it!
Terrence A. Friedman,
Founder and President,
Victoria National Golf Club

175

Cranberry Lemon Cake with Lemon Glaze

Kitchen Affairs

176

Cake

1/4 cup sugar	4 eggs
1 (2-layer) package lemon cake mix with pudding	1 teaspoon mace
3 ounces cream cheese, softened	1 1/4 cups finely chopped cranberries
3/4 cup milk	1/2 cup finely chopped walnuts

Glaze

2 cups confectioners' sugar	1 to 2 teaspoons grated lemon zest
1 tablespoon butter, softened	
2 to 3 tablespoons fresh lemon juice	

For the cake, generously grease a 12-cup bundt or kugelhopf pan and sprinkle with the sugar. Combine the cake mix, cream cheese, milk, eggs and mace in a mixing bowl, mixing at medium speed for 4 to 5 minutes or until of a uniform consistency. Fold in the cranberries and walnuts. Pour the batter into the prepared pan. Bake at 350 degrees for 40 minutes or until a wooden pick inserted into the center of the cake comes out clean. Cool in the pan for 10 to 15 minutes. Invert onto a wire rack or serving plate to cool completely.

For the glaze, combine the confectioners' sugar and butter in a small bowl. Add the lemon juice gradually to achieve the desired consistency, stirring until smooth. Stir in the lemon zest. Drizzle over the cooled cake. *Yield: 16 servings.*

NOTE: USE A FOOD PROCESSOR TO FINELY CHOP THE CRANBERRIES AND WALNUTS. (THERE'S NO NEED TO WASH THE CONTAINER IN BETWEEN.)

Gooey Butter Cake

1 (2-layer) package yellow cake mix
1/2 cup (1 stick) margarine, melted
2 eggs
3 3/4 cups confectioners' sugar

8 ounces cream cheese, softened
2 eggs
1 1/2 tablespoons vanilla extract
1/4 cup confectioners' sugar

Mix the cake mix, margarine and 2 eggs in a bowl with a fork. Press into a well-greased 9×13-inch cake pan.

Beat 3 3/4 cup confectioners' sugar, the cream cheese, 2 eggs and vanilla in a mixing bowl, mixing at medium-high speed for 5 minutes. Spread over the cake mixture. Bake at 350 degrees for 35 minutes or until golden brown. Cool in the pan. Sprinkle with 1/4 cup confectioners' sugar. *Yield*: 12 *to* 14 *servings*.

Absolutely Sinful Chocolate Cake

1 (2-layer) package German chocolate cake mix
1 (14-ounce) package caramels

1 (14-ounce) can sweetened condensed milk
2 2/3 cups chocolate chips

Prepare the cake mix using the package directions. Pour half the batter into a greased and floured 9-inch square cake pan. Bake at the oven temperature specified on the package for 20 to 25 minutes or until gooey.

Combine the caramels and sweetened condensed milk in a saucepan. Cook until the caramels melt, stirring constantly. Pour over the baked cake. Sprinkle with the chocolate chips. Pour the remaining cake batter over the top, spreading evenly. Bake for 30 minutes or until the cake tests done. Cool in the pan. Cut into squares. Reheat in the microwave oven if desired and serve warm with vanilla ice cream and drizzles of Kahlúa. *Yield*: 15 *servings*.

MOKAZ Coconut Cake with Coconut Cream Cheese Frosting

What, you may be asking, is MOKAZ? MOKAZ is an illustrious Evansville group that began in 1970 when five couples dining together realized that one spouse in each couple celebrated a birthday on consecutive days in February. The five members of MOKAZ include Mary Jane Miles (M), Rosemary O'Daniel (O), Jack Kinkel (K), Jane Annakin (A), and Ted Zeimer (Z). The five couples recognized the unique opportunity to celebrate each other's birthdays and decided to commemorate the week with annually planned parties.

(continued on next page)

178

Cake

1 (2-layer) package yellow cake mix
1 (4-ounce) package vanilla instant pudding mix
1¹/₂ cups water

4 eggs
¹/₄ cup vegetable oil
2 cups shredded coconut
1 cup chopped walnuts or pecans

Frosting

4 tablespoons butter or margarine
2 cups shredded coconut
8 ounces cream cheese, softened

2 teaspoons milk
3¹/₂ cups sifted confectioners' sugar
¹/₂ teaspoon vanilla extract

For the cake, blend the cake mix, pudding mix, water, eggs and oil in a large mixing bowl. Beat at medium speed for 4 minutes. Stir in the coconut and walnuts. Pour into 3 greased and floured 9-inch round cake pans. Bake at 350 degrees for 35 minutes or until the layers test done. Cool in the pans for 15 minutes. Remove to wire racks to cool completely.

For the frosting, melt 2 tablespoons of the butter in a skillet. Add the coconut. Cook over low heat until golden brown, stirring constantly. Spread on paper towels to cool.

Cream the remaining 2 tablespoons butter and cream cheese in a mixing bowl. Add the milk and confectioners' sugar alternately, beating well after each addition. Add the vanilla. Stir in 1³/₄ cups of the cooked coconut. Spread between the layers and over the top and side of the cake. Sprinkle with the remaining coconut. *Yield: 20 servings.*

Lorenzo's Chocolate Bourbon Cake

Lorenzo's Breads and Bistro

1³/4 cups hot brewed coffee
¹/4 cup bourbon
1 cup (2 sticks) unsalted butter, cut into small pieces
5 ounces unsweetened chocolate, cut into small pieces
2 cups sugar
2 cups flour
1 teaspoon baking soda
Pinch of salt
2 eggs, at room temperature
1 teaspoon vanilla extract

Combine the coffee, bourbon, butter and chocolate in a large metal bowl. Let stand, covered, until the butter and chocolate are completely melted. Whisk until blended. Whisk in the sugar. Cool to room temperature.

Sift the flour, baking soda and salt together in a bowl. Whisk half at a time into the chocolate mixture. Whisk in the eggs and vanilla. Pour into 2 greased and floured 8- or 9-inch round cake pans. Bake at 275 degrees for 50 minutes or until a wooden pick inserted into the center comes out clean. Cool in the pans on wire racks. (May be used immediately or refrigerated in the pans, covered with plastic wrap. It is easier to decorate a cool cake.)

To remove from the pans, run a knife around the inside edges and invert, tapping on the bottoms of the pans to loosen the layers. If the layers stick slightly, place the pans over low heat, moving them constantly to prevent burning. Invert again and the layers should slide out. Spread your favorite icing between the layers and over the top and side of the cake. *Yield: 12 servings.*

NOTE: WE OFTEN ICE THIS CAKE WITH A VERY BASIC CHOCOLATE BUTTERCREAM ICING OR CHOCOLATE GANACHE.

The five-day celebration has included costumed theme parties, personalized MOKAZ gifts, an official song, and even vacations. Over the years, the families of this group have been forced to endure this week of festivities. Interestingly, as the MOKAZ tradition became more outlandish, the spouses (in self-defense perhaps) adopted the name ZAKOM. What a wonderful tribute to friendship and fun!

179

Chocolate Praline Cake with
Chocolate Ganache and Praline Frosting

Cake

1 cup (2 sticks) butter or margarine	1 teaspoon baking soda
1 cup water	1 teaspoon vanilla extract
$1/4$ cup baking cocoa	2 cups sugar
$1/2$ cup buttermilk	2 cups flour
2 eggs	$1/2$ teaspoon salt

Ganache

2 cups (12 ounces) semisweet chocolate chips	$1/4$ cup ($1/2$ stick) butter or margarine, cut into pieces
$1/3$ cup heavy cream	

Frosting

1 cup packed brown sugar	1 teaspoon vanilla extract
$1/4$ cup ($1/2$ stick) butter or margarine	1 cup chopped pecans, toasted
$1/3$ cup heavy cream	Pecan halves (about 20)
1 cup confectioners' sugar	

180

For the cake, coat three 9-inch round cake pans with nonstick cooking spray. Line the pans with waxed paper. Combine the butter, water and baking cocoa in a small saucepan. Cook over low heat until the butter melts and the mixture is smooth, stirring constantly. Remove from the heat.

Beat the buttermilk, eggs, baking soda and vanilla in a mixing bowl at medium speed until smooth. Add the butter mixture. Beat until well blended. Combine the sugar, flour and salt in a bowl. Add to the butter mixture gradually, beating until blended. Pour evenly into the prepared pans. Bake at 350 degrees for 18 to 22 minutes or until set. Cool in the pans on wire racks for 10 minutes. Remove to wire racks to cool completely.

For the ganache, place the chocolate chips and cream in a microwave-safe bowl. Microwave on Medium for 2 to 3 minutes or until the chocolate melts. Whisk until smooth. Whisk in the butter gradually. Cool until the mixture reaches a spreading consistency, whisking frequently. Spread $1/2$ cup of the ganache between the layers and the remainder over the side of the cake.

For the frosting, bring the brown sugar, butter and cream to a boil in a 2-quart saucepan over medium heat, stirring frequently. Boil for 1 minute. Remove from the heat. Whisk in the confectioners' sugar and vanilla until smooth. Add the chopped pecans. Stir gently for 3 to 5 minutes or until the mixture begins to cool and thicken slightly. Immediately pour over the top center of the cake in a slow stream, spreading the frosting to the edge and allowing some to run down the side. Decorate the top edge of the cake with the pecan halves. *Yield: 12 servings.*

Chocolate Chip Cake

1 (2-layer) package chocolate cake mix
1 (4-ounce) package chocolate instant
    pudding mix
3/4 cup sour cream
1/2 cup hot water

1/2 cup vegetable oil
3 eggs
3 cups (18 ounces) semisweet chocolate
    chips
3/4 cup heavy cream

Beat the cake mix, pudding mix, sour cream, hot water, oil and eggs in a mixing bowl. Stir in 1 1/2 cups of the chocolate chips. Pour into a greased and floured 10-inch fluted tube pan. Bake at 350 degrees for 1 hour or until a wooden pick inserted into the center of the cake comes out clean. Cool in the pan for 10 minutes. Invert onto a wire rack to cool completely.

Heat the cream in a saucepan to a simmer. Remove from the heat. Whisk in the remaining 1 1/2 cups chocolate chips until melted and smooth. Drizzle over the cake. *Yield: 16 servings.*

Milk Chocolate Bar Cake

1 (2-layer) package Swiss chocolate
    cake mix
8 ounces cream cheese, softened
1 cup confectioners' sugar

1/2 cup sugar
10 (2-ounce) milk chocolate candy bars
    with almonds
12 ounces whipped topping

Prepare the cake mix using the package directions. Pour into 3 greased 8-inch round cake pans. Bake at 325 degrees for 20 to 25 minutes or until a wooden pick inserted in the center comes out clean. Cool in the pans for 10 minutes. Remove to wire racks to cool completely.

Beat the cream cheese, confectioners' sugar and sugar in a mixing bowl at medium speed until creamy. Finely chop 8 of the candy bars. Fold the cream cheese mixture and chopped candy into the whipped topping in a bowl. Spread between the layers and over the top and side of the cake. Chop the remaining 2 candy bars and sprinkle over the top. Refrigerate any leftovers. *Yield: 12 servings.*

Italian Love Cake

1 (2-layer) package fudge marble cake mix
30 ounces low-fat ricotta cheese
¾ cup sugar
4 eggs
1 teaspoon vanilla extract

1 (4-ounce) package milk chocolate
    instant pudding mix
1 cup skim milk
8 ounces low-fat whipped topping

Prepare the cake mix using the package directions. Pour the batter into a greased and floured 9×13-inch cake pan; set aside.

Combine the cheese, sugar, eggs and vanilla in a large mixing bowl, beating until smooth. Spoon over the cake batter. Bake at 350 degrees for 1 hour. Cool in the pan.

Whisk the pudding mix and milk in a bowl. Fold in the whipped topping. Spread over the cooled cake. Chill, covered with plastic wrap, until ready to serve. *Yield: 16 to 20 servings.*

NOTE: MAY SUBSTITUTE CHOCOLATE OR DEVIL'S FOOD CAKE MIX FOR THE FUDGE MARBLE CAKE MIX. MAY MAKE AHEAD SINCE THIS CAKE KEEPS WELL IN THE REFRIGERATOR.

Crunchy Caramel Apple Pie

1 unbaked (9-inch) deep-dish pie shell
¼ cup sugar
3 tablespoons flour
1 teaspoon cinnamon
⅛ teaspoon salt
5½ cups sliced peeled apples
½ cup packed brown sugar

½ cup (1 stick) butter
½ cup flour
½ cup quick-cooking oats
½ cup chopped pecans
⅓ cup caramel or butterscotch ice cream
    topping

Crimp the edges of the pie shell. Combine the sugar, 3 tablespoons flour, cinnamon and salt in a bowl. Stir in the apples. Spoon into the pie shell.

Mix the brown sugar, butter, ½ cup flour and oats in a bowl with a pastry blender until crumbly. Sprinkle over the apples. Bake at 375 degrees for 20 to 30 minutes. Cover the pie with foil. Bake for 20 minutes. Uncover the pie. Sprinkle with the pecans and drizzle with the caramel topping. Cool on
a wire rack. Serve with ice cream. *Yield: 8 servings.*

Chocolate Banana Pudding Pie

4 ounces semisweet chocolate
2 tablespoons milk
1 tablespoon margarine
1 (9-inch) graham cracker pie shell
2 medium bananas, sliced

2³/4 cups cold milk
2 (4-ounce) packages banana instant
 pudding mix
1¹/2 cups whipped topping

Place the chocolate, milk and margarine in a medium microwave-safe bowl. Microwave on High for 1 to 1¹/2 minutes, stirring every 30 seconds. Stir until the chocolate is completely melted. Spread evenly in the pie shell. Chill for 30 minutes or until the chocolate is firm.

Arrange the banana slices over the chocolate. Combine the milk and pudding mixes in a large bowl. Whisk for 1 minute. Let stand for 5 minutes. Spoon over the bananas. Spread with the whipped topping. Chill for 4 hours. *Yield: 8 servings.*

Pear Cheddar Pie

Filling

4 or 5 large ripe Bartlett
pears, peeled, thinly sliced
¹/3 cup sugar

1 tablespoon cornstarch
¹/8 teaspoon salt
1 refrigerator pastry crust

Topping

¹/2 cup flour
¹/4 cup sugar
¹/4 teaspoon salt
¹/2 cup (2 ounces) shredded sharp
Cheddar cheese

¹/4 cup (¹/2 stick) butter, melted, cooled
 slightly

For the filling, combine the pears, sugar, cornstarch and salt in a bowl, mixing carefully. Unfold the pastry crust into a 9-inch pie plate. Pour the filling into the crust.

For the topping, whisk the flour, sugar and salt in a bowl. Add the cheese and mix with your fingers. Add the butter and mix with your fingers until crumbly. Sprinkle evenly over the filling. Bake at 425 degrees for 25 to 35 minutes or until the crust is golden brown and the cheese is melted. Cool for 10 minutes on a wire rack. Serve warm with vanilla ice cream if desired. *Yield: 8 servings.*

Easy Apple Dumplings

2 (8-count) cans crescent rolls
2 cooking apples, peeled,
each cut into 8 slices
1¹/₂ cups sugar

1 cup (2 sticks) butter, melted
1 teaspoon cinnamon
1 (12-ounce) can lemon-lime soda

Separate the crescent roll dough into 16 triangles. Place 1 apple slice on each triangle. Roll up each triangle, starting from the wide edge. Place in a 9×13-inch baking pan. Combine the sugar, butter and cinnamon in a bowl. Pour the butter mixture and soda over the dumplings. Bake at 350 degrees for 45 minutes. *Yield:* 16 *servings.*

Peaches and Cream Pie

³/₄ cup flour
1 (4-ounce) package vanilla instant
pudding mix
¹/₂ cup milk
3 tablespoons margarine, softened
1 egg

1 teaspoon baking powder
¹/₂ teaspoon salt
1 (15-ounce) can sliced peaches
8 ounces cream cheese, softened
¹/₂ cup sugar
2 tablespoons cinnamon-sugar

Combine the flour, pudding mix, milk, margarine, egg, baking powder and salt in a bowl. Spread on the bottom and up the side of a greased 9-inch pie plate.

Drain the peaches, reserving 3 tablespoons juice. Arrange the peach slices in a spiral over the crust. Combine the cream cheese, reserved peach juice and sugar in a bowl. Spread over the peach slices. Sprinkle with the cinnamon-sugar. Place the pie plate on a baking sheet. Bake at 350 degrees for 45 minutes or until set. *Yield:* 8 *servings.*

Chocolate Bourbon Pie

½ cup (1 stick) butter	1 cup (6 ounces) semisweet
1 cup sugar	chocolate chips
2 eggs, beaten	1 cup walnuts, chopped
1 teaspoon vanilla extract	1 to 2 tablespoons bourbon
½ cup flour	1 unbaked (8-inch) pie shell

Place the butter in a microwave-safe bowl. Microwave on High until melted. Whisk in the sugar until blended. Whisk in the eggs and vanilla. Add the flour and mix well. Stir in the chocolate chips and walnuts. Stir in the bourbon. Pour into the pie shell.

Bake at 350 degrees for 35 to 40 minutes. Cool to almost room temperature before cutting. *Yield: 8 servings.*

Cinnamon Sensations

1 large loaf thinly sliced	1 egg yolk
bread, crusts trimmed	¾ cup packed brown sugar
8 ounces cream cheese,	½ teaspoon cinnamon
softened	¾ cup (1½ sticks) margarine,
½ cup sugar	melted

Roll each bread slice as thinly as possible. Combine the cream cheese, sugar and egg yolk in a bowl. Spread over 1 side of each bread slice. Roll up each slice, pressing the edge to seal.

Combine the brown sugar and cinnamon in a shallow dish. Dip each roll in the margarine, then roll in the sugar mixture. Place the rolls on waxed paper and freeze for 4 to 12 hours.

Slice each roll crosswise into 3 or 4 pieces. Place on greased baking sheets. Bake at 350 degrees for 8 to 10 minutes. Serve hot or cold with sour cream for dipping. *Yield: 50 servings.*

When I was a little girl, I loved to watch my grandmother make pies. She always had leftover pie pastry, which she made into "snails" for us. She rolled out the remaining pastry, brushed the top with melted butter, and sprinkled it with sugar and cinnamon. Then she rolled up the dough, sliced it into "snails," and baked them for about 10 minutes along with the pies. We could hardly let them cool before we'd gobble them up! I continue the tradition today with my children.

Kirsten Wagmeister

Bread Pudding with Whiskey Sauce

Haub Steak House

186

Whiskey Sauce
³/4 cup sugar
5 tablespoons butter, softened
1 egg, beaten
2 ounces whiskey

Bread Pudding
5 cups dry bread pieces
4 cups milk
2 cups sugar
3 eggs
2 tablespoons vanilla extract
1 cup raisins
3 tablespoons butter

For *the whiskey sauce,* cream the sugar and butter in a saucepan with a hand mixer. Bring almost to a boil. Stir in the egg. Cook for 1 minute. Remove from the heat; cool. Stir in the whiskey; set aside.

For *the bread pudding,* soak the bread pieces in the milk in a bowl, crushing with your hands until well mixed. Add the sugar, eggs, vanilla and raisins and stir well. Melt the butter in a 9×13-inch baking dish in a 325-degree oven. Pour the bread mixture into the dish. Bake at 325 degrees for 1 hour or until a knife inserted near the center comes out clean. Cool completely. Cut into squares. Place each square on an ovenproof or microwave-safe dessert plate. Top with the Whiskey Sauce. Heat under the broiler or in the microwave oven. *Yield: 10 servings.*

Spumoni Cheesecake

Crust

1 cup finely ground pistachios $^1/_3$ cup butter or margarine, melted
$^3/_4$ cup finely crushed graham crackers

Filling

24 ounces cream cheese, softened   2 eggs
1 cup sugar   1 egg yolk
2 tablespoons flour   2 tablespoons milk
1 teaspoon vanilla extract   2 tablespoons amaretto

Topping

1 cup whipping cream   4 tablespoons ($^1/_4$ cup) grated semisweet
$1^1/_2$ tablespoons confectioners'   chocolate
sugar   Finely chopped pistachios
$^1/_2$ teaspoon vanilla extract   Sliced strawberries

Grease the bottom and $1^1/_4$ inches up the side of a 9-inch springform pan; set aside.

For the crust, combine the pistachios and graham crackers in a medium mixing bowl. Stir in the butter. Press onto the bottom and about $1^1/_4$ inches up the side of the prepared pan. Chill, covered, until ready to use.

For the filling, beat the cream cheese, sugar, flour and vanilla in a large mixing bowl until combined. Add the eggs and egg yolk, beating at low speed just until combined. Stir in the milk and amaretto. Pour into the chilled crust. Place the pan in a shallow baking pan. Bake at 375 degrees for 35 to 40 minutes or until the center appears nearly set when the pan is shaken. Cool in the pan on a wire rack for 15 minutes. Loosen the crust from the side of the pan. Cool for 30 minutes longer. Remove the side of the pan. Cool completely. Chill, covered, for 4 to 24 hours.

For the topping, just before serving, beat the cream, confectioners' sugar and vanilla in a mixing bowl until stiff peaks form. Sprinkle the cheesecake with 3 tablespoons of the chocolate. Pipe the whipped cream over the top. Sprinkle with the remaining 1 tablespoon chocolate and pistachios. Arrange strawberries on the top. Yield: 12 to 16 servings.

Tiramisu Cheesecake

Crust

³/₄ cup finely crushed chocolate wafer cookies (about 13 cookies)

2 tablespoons butter, melted
6 ladyfingers, split

Filling

1 teaspoon instant espresso powder or instant coffee crystals
2 tablespoons rum, brandy or milk
8 ounces mascarpone cheese or cream cheese, softened

16 ounces cream cheese, softened
1 cup sugar
1 tablespoon cornstarch
1 teaspoon vanilla extract
3 eggs

Topping

1 cup sour cream   Grated semisweet chocolate (optional)

For the crust, combine the cookies and butter in a bowl. Press onto the bottom of an ungreased 9-inch springform pan. Cut the split ladyfingers crosswise into halves. Arrange the ladyfingers rounded side out and cut side down around the side of the pan; set aside.

For the filling, dissolve the espresso powder in the rum in a bowl; set aside. Beat the mascarpone cheese and cream cheese in a medium mixing bowl until combined. Add the sugar gradually, beating at medium to high speed until smooth. Beat in the cornstarch and vanilla. Add the eggs. Beat at low speed just until combined. Stir in the coffee mixture. Pour into the crust. Place the pan in a shallow baking pan. Bake at 350 degrees for 45 to 50 minutes or until the center appears nearly set when the pan is gently shaken.

For the topping, stir the sour cream. Spoon gently over the top of the hot cheesecake, spreading carefully to within 1 inch of the edge. Cool in the pan on a wire rack for 15 minutes. Loosen the ladyfingers from the side of the pan carefully with a narrow metal spatula. Cool for 1 hour. Chill, covered, for at least 4 hours. Remove the side of the pan. Sprinkle with chocolate before serving if desired. *Yield: 12 servings.*

Cookie Dough Cheesecake

2 (18-ounce) packages chocolate chip
cookie dough or sugar cookie dough
32 ounces cream cheese, softened

1 cup sugar
4 eggs
1 teaspoon vanilla extract

Press half the cookie dough onto the bottom and up the sides of a 9-inch springform pan. Mix the cream cheese, sugar, eggs and vanilla in a bowl. Pour into the pan. Place chunks of the remaining cookie dough over the top. Bake at 350 degrees for 30 to 45 minutes or until the center is set. Cool for 10 minutes. Run a knife around the edge to loosen. Chill for at least 6 hours before removing from the pan. *Yield*: 15 *servings*.

Chocolate Éclair Dessert

2 (4-ounce) packages vanilla instant
pudding mix
3 cups milk
1 teaspoon vanilla extract
8 ounces whipped topping
24 whole graham crackers

$1/3$ cup butter
$1/4$ cup water
1 tablespoon (heaping) baking cocoa
$2 1/2$ cups confectioners' sugar
1 teaspoon vanilla extract

Combine the pudding mixes, milk and 1 teaspoon vanilla in a bowl. Fold in the whipped topping. Layer $1/3$ of the graham crackers and $1/2$ of the pudding mixture alternately in a 9×13-inch baking pan, ending with the graham crackers.

Heat the butter and water in a saucepan over low heat until the butter is melted. Stir in the baking cocoa. Remove from the heat. Stir in the confectioners' sugar gradually. Whisk until smooth. Stir in 1 teaspoon vanilla. Spread over the top layer of graham crackers. Chill, covered, until set. *Yield*: 15 *servings*.

NOTE: MAY ALSO BE FROZEN.

White Velvet Mousse

1 envelope unflavored gelatin
³/₄ cup sugar
1 pint heavy cream

2 cups sour cream
1 tablespoon vanilla extract
Frozen or fresh raspberries

Soften the gelatin in a small amount of cold water. Combine the gelatin mixture and sugar in a saucepan. Stir in the cream. Let stand for 5 minutes. Cook over low heat for 5 minutes or until the gelatin is completely dissolved. Remove from the heat; cool completely.

Stir in the sour cream and vanilla and mix well. Pour into a serving bowl. Chill, covered, for 2 to 12 hours. Serve topped with raspberries. *Yield: 8 servings.*

Crispy Oat Crunchies

1 cup (2 sticks) butter, softened
1 cup sugar
1 cup packed brown sugar
1 egg
1 cup vegetable oil
1 teaspoon vanilla extract
3¹/₂ cups flour

1 teaspoon baking soda
¹/₂ teaspoon salt
1 cup rolled oats
1 cup crushed cornflakes
¹/₂ cup flaked coconut
¹/₂ cup chopped walnuts

Cream the butter, sugar and brown sugar in a mixing bowl at medium speed. Add the egg and beat well. Add the oil and vanilla. Beat in a mixture of the flour, baking soda and salt. Stir in the oats, cornflakes, coconut and walnuts. Shape into 1-inch balls. Place 2 inches apart on ungreased cookie sheets. Flatten each ball with the tines of a fork. Bake at 350 degrees for 15 minutes. Cool slightly on the cookie sheets. Remove to a wire rack to cool completely. *Yield: 7 dozen cookies.*

Famous "O" Cookies

1 cup (2 sticks) butter or margarine, softened
1 cup sugar
1 cup packed light brown sugar
2 eggs
1 cup chunky peanut butter
1½ cups flour
1 teaspoon baking powder
1 teaspoon baking soda
1 teaspoon vanilla extract
¼ teaspoon salt
2½ cups rolled oats
1 cup (6 ounces) chocolate chips

Cream the butter, sugar and brown sugar in a mixing bowl until light and fluffy. Add the eggs and mix well. Mix in the peanut butter. Add the flour, baking powder, baking soda, vanilla and salt and mix well. Stir in the oats and chocolate chips. Drop by rounded tablespoonfuls 2 inches apart onto an ungreased cookie sheet. Bake at 350 degrees for 10 to 12 minutes. (Cookies will not appear to be done.) Cool on a wire rack. *Yield: about 4½ dozen cookies.*

NOTE: USE A MEDIUM COOKIE SCOOP THAT MEASURES ABOUT **2 TABLESPOONS FOR PERFECT 2½-INCH COOKIES.**

My mother made everything from scratch: biscuits, cakes, brownies, etc. Cookies were a constant in our house—fresh or frozen, our family always had cookies to enjoy. Now that I'm married (however, not on a farm!), I, too, have continued with homemade cookies in my house. Store-made cookies are just not found in my home, so I was truly mortified when our little neighbor boy sold only store-made cookie dough for his fund-raiser. I told him that I had never bought cookie dough, and he couldn't believe it! Out of the goodness of my heart, however, I purchased some, and my family really enjoyed those cookies! I have not bought any more cookie dough to this day . . . old habits are hard to break!

Lynn Ogle

Fondant Cookies with Fondant Icing

Cookies

¹/₂ cup (1 stick) butter or margarine, softened

1 cup sugar

1 egg

2 envelopes premelted unsweetened chocolate, or 2 ounces unsweetened chocolate, melted

¹/₃ cup milk

1 teaspoon vanilla extract

2 cups flour

1 cup chopped pecans (optional)

¹/₂ teaspoon baking powder

¹/₂ teaspoon salt

Icing

2 cups confectioners' sugar

2 tablespoons light corn syrup

2 tablespoons (about) hot water

1 teaspoon almond extract

Red food coloring

¹/₄ teaspoon peppermint extract

Green food coloring

For the cookies, beat the butter, sugar, egg, chocolate, milk and vanilla in a large mixing bowl. Mix in the flour, pecans, baking powder and salt at low speed until a soft dough forms, scraping down the side of the bowl constantly.

Chill, covered, for 1 to 2 hours or until firm enough to handle. Shape by rounded teaspoonfuls into balls. Place 2 inches apart on an ungreased cookie sheet. Bake at 400 degrees for about 7 minutes. Cool on a wire rack.

For the icing, combine the confectioners' sugar, corn syrup and water in a small bowl. (If the icing is too thin, add more confectioners' sugar to thicken.) Pour half the icing into another bowl. Stir the almond extract and a desired amount of red food coloring into half the icing. Stir the peppermint extract and a desired amount of green food coloring into the other half. Swirl the tops of the cookies into either the red or green icing. *Yield: about 4 dozen cookies.*

Cranberry Crumb Bars

Crust

1½ cups flour
1½ cups quick-cooking oats
¾ cup packed brown sugar
½ cup walnuts, finely
   chopped

½ teaspoon salt
¾ cup (1½ sticks) unsalted
   butter, softened
1 tablespoon cold water

Filling

2¼ cups fresh cranberries   ¾ cup red raspberry jam

Line a 9-inch square baking pan with 2 crisscrossed pieces of foil, letting the ends of the foil extend over the sides of the pan; set aside.

For the crust, combine the flour, oats, brown sugar, walnuts and salt in a medium bowl. Add the butter and mix until clumpy. Press about 2½ cups evenly over the bottom of the prepared pan. Bake at 375 degrees for 10 minutes or until golden brown. Add the water to the remaining crust mixture and toss to mix.

For the filling, combine the cranberries and jam in a small bowl. Drop by spoonfuls over the crust and spread evenly. Crumble the remaining crust mixture over the top. Bake at 375 degrees for 40 minutes or until the topping is golden brown and the filling is bubbly. Cool completely in the pan. Remove from the pan by lifting out with the foil. Cut into squares. Yield: about 20 bars.

NOTE: MAY SUBSTITUTE RASPBERRIES FOR THE CRANBERRIES.

Cinnamon-Sugar Pecans

2½ cups large pecan halves

1 cup sugar

1/2 cup water

1 teaspoon salt

1 teaspoon cinnamon

1½ teaspoons vanilla

Toast the pecans on a baking sheet at 375 degrees for 15 minutes, stirring frequently; set aside. Combine the sugar, water, salt and cinnamon in a heavy saucepan. Cook, uncovered, over high heat to 236 degrees on a candy thermometer, soft-ball stage; do not stir. Remove from the heat. Stir in the vanilla. Add the pecans and stir gently until coated and creamy. Pour onto a greased platter and spread out to separate.

Yield: 2½ cups

Grasshopper

¾ ounce crème de menthe

¾ ounce crème de cacao

¾ ounce half-and-half

Blend or shake the crème de menthe, crème de cacao and half-and-half with cracked ice.

Strain into a chilled Champagne or cocktail glass.

A couple of these will have you hoppin'!

Yield: 1 serving

Crème de Menthe Bars

½ cup (1 stick) unsalted butter
½ cup baking cocoa
½ cup confectioners' sugar
1 egg, beaten
1 teaspoon vanilla extract
2 cups chocolate wafer cookie crumbs

½ cup (1 stick) unsalted butter, softened
¼ cup crème de menthe
3 cups confectioners' sugar
¼ cup (½ stick) unsalted butter
1½ cups (9 ounces) semisweet chocolate chips

Heat ½ cup butter and the baking cocoa in a saucepan until the butter is melted, stirring until smooth. Remove from the heat. Add ½ cup confectioners' sugar, the egg and vanilla. Stir in the cookie crumbs. Press onto the bottom of an ungreased 9×13-inch baking pan; set aside.

Combine ½ cup butter and the crème de menthe in a mixing bowl. Beat in 3 cups confectioners' sugar. Add some green food coloring if more color is desired. Spread over the crust. Chill, covered, for at least 1 hour.

Melt ¼ cup butter and the chocolate chips in a saucepan or in a microwave-safe bowl in a microwave oven. Spread over the top. Chill, covered, for 24 hours. Let stand at room temperature for 10 minutes before cutting into bars. Yield: 2 dozen bars.

Chocolate Peanut Butter Squares

1¹/₂ cups graham cracker crumbs
3 cups confectioners' sugar
¹/₂ cup (1 stick) butter, melted
1 cup natural creamy peanut butter
2 cups (12 ounces) semisweet chocolate chips

Combine the graham cracker crumbs and confectioners' sugar in a large bowl and mix well. Stir in the butter and peanut butter, mixing well. (The mixture will be very thick.) Spread in an ungreased 9×13-inch baking pan, pressing firmly into an even layer. Press waxed paper or parchment paper over the surface. Chill for 45 to 60 minutes or until set.

Melt the chocolate chips in the top of a double boiler over simmering water over low heat, stirring constantly with a wooden spoon until smooth. Remove the waxed paper from the peanut butter mixture. Spread the melted chocolate over the top. Let stand for 15 minutes or until the chocolate is firm. Cut into 1- to 2-inch squares. *Yield: 3 dozen squares.*

Ghostly Good Cookies

Here's an easy Halloween treat that children will have fun making and eating!

1 (24-ounce) package vanilla-flavor almond bark
1 (16-ounce) package peanut-shaped sandwich cookies
40 (about) miniature chocolate chips

Melt the almond bark in a microwave-safe bowl in the microwave oven or in a saucepan over medium heat. Dip the cookies into the melted bark to cover completely. Place on waxed paper. Place 2 miniature chocolate chips on top of each cookie for "eyes." Let cool.

Caramel Brownies

1 (2-layer) package German chocolate
cake mix
1/2 cup (1 stick) butter, melted
1/3 cup evaporated milk

2 cups (12 ounces) chocolate chips
1 (12-ounce) package caramels
1/3 cup evaporated milk

Combine the cake mix, butter and 1/3 cup evaporated milk in a bowl. Press half the mixture into a greased and floured 9×13-inch baking pan. Bake at 350 degrees for 6 minutes. Remove from the oven. Sprinkle with the chocolate chips.

Place the caramels and 1/3 cup evaporated milk in a microwave-safe bowl. Microwave until the caramels are melted; stir until blended. Spread over the chocolate chips. Crumble the remaining cake mixture over the caramel. Bake at 350 degrees for 15 minutes. Let cool before cutting. Yield: 15 *servings*.

Fabulous Fudge

2 cups (12 ounces) semisweet
chocolate chips
1 (13-ounce) jar marshmallow creme
2 cups chopped pecans

2 teaspoons vanilla extract
5 cups sugar
1 (12-ounce) can evaporated milk
1 cup (2 sticks) butter

Combine the chocolate chips, marshmallow creme, pecans and vanilla in a mixing bowl; set aside.
Combine the sugar, evaporated milk and butter in a large saucepan. Bring to to a boil. Boil for 15 minutes, stirring frequently. Continue cooking to 234 degrees on a candy thermometer, soft-ball stage. Pour over the chocolate chip mixture. Beat at high speed until creamy. Pour into a buttered 9×13-inch baking pan. Let stand for 3 to 4 hours or until set. Yield: 100 (1-*inch*) *pieces*.

Nana's Hot Fudge Sauce with Easy Vanilla Ice Cream

Fudge Sauce

1/4 cup (1/2 stick) butter	1 cup sugar
1 ounce unsweetened chocolate	1 cup evaporated milk
1 ounce semisweet chocolate	1 teaspoon vanilla extract

Ice Cream

1 pint half-and-half	2 cups sugar
1 cup heavy cream	1 tablespoon vanilla extract
1 (12-ounce) can evaporated milk	Milk

For the fudge sauce, melt the butter, unsweetened chocolate and semisweet chocolate in a saucepan. Remove from the heat. Add the sugar and mix well. Add the evaporated milk and vanilla and mix well. Return to the heat. Boil until a ball can form on the end of a spoon. Pour into a serving dish; cool.

For the ice cream, combine the half-and-half, cream, evaporated milk, sugar and vanilla in a 6-quart ice cream freezer container; add milk to the fill line. Freeze using the manufacturer's directions. Serve with Fudge Sauce. *Yield: 24 servings.*

My grandmother, Edith Paschen Gross (Nana), has always made this incredible hot fudge. On special occasions, Nana would put it into small syrup dispensers and wrap them in tissue paper, leaving only the handles sticking out. Whenever we saw those little handles, we always knew we were in for a real treat! Nana is an amazing mother of 4, grandmother of 18, and great-grandmother of 26 . . . and still has the energy of a 21-year-old! She is my role model and is dearly loved and admired by everyone in our family.

Michele Kinkel

Contributing Chefs
and Restaurants

Café Driftwood

Evansville Country Club,
Chef Kenneth Thompson, C.S.C.

Evansville Living Magazine

The Flying Pigs

Haub Steak House

Kennel Club of Evansville

Kitchen Affairs,
Mike and Shelly Sackett

Lorenzo's Breads and Bistro

Maxine's Café and Bakery

Oak Meadow Golf Club, Inc.
Pam Heironimus, Executive Chef

The Old Mill

The Pasta Grill

Raffi's Restaurant

Rolling Hills Country Club,
Executive Chef Michael Dell, C.E.C.

Victoria National Golf Club,
Chef Douglas Rennie, C.E.C.

Recipe Contributors

ABCDEFGHI

Kellie Adler
Kristie Alexander
Kristie M. Alexander
Peggy Annakin
Suzanna Annakin
Ann Arosteguy
Cindi Ball
Kathy Barnett
Allison Beck
Cinda Beeler
Cindy Behrens
Terri Betz
Gwen Bizal
April Boeke
Stephanie Boyer
Elyse Brasseale
Suzette Broshears
Francesca Brougham
Joan Brougham
Jean Brubeck
Rachel Buchta
Sheila Coldwell
Barbara Compton
Suzie Consoer
Angie Cooley
Beverly Cross
Allene Doddoli
Amanda Eagleston
Patricia Eble
Mildred Engle
Ann Enlow
Michelle Eykamp
Rita Eykamp
Jo Davidson Frauenhoff
Kelly Fries
Christine Gest
Melissa Gillenwater
Jenny Godwin
Bernie Goebel
Lori Goris

Susan Grabert
Mindy Graper
Tessie Grimm
Jane Grizzell
Edith Paschen Gross
Betsy Gurtcheff
Jingle Igleheart Hagey
Diane Hagler
Shara Hammet
Vicki Hart
Kristen Haynie
Sandy Haywood
Kimberly Haywood-Pfender
Carolyn Helm
Allison Hemmerlein
Lou Honningford
Joyce Hubbard
Bethany Hunt
Lori Hupfer
Toscha Hurm

JKLMNOPQ

Linda Johnson
Christina Jones
Janet Keller
Sandy Kelley
Linda Kinkel
Michele Kinkel
Amy Kolleck
Jean Korb
Donna Logan
Allison Lueking
Joelle Lynch
Karen Magan
Brittany Mason
Wendy McCormick
Jean McGuire
Kathy McMurray
Karen Meacham
Mary Jane Miles

Rachael Miles
Andrea Miller
Sara Miller
Nancy Mitchell
Kimberly Moman
Tamara Moore
Nancy Morgan
Stephanie Morris
Lynn Muehlbauer
Mary Kay Muehlbauer
Linda Myers
Jamie Neel
Suzanne Nicholson
Karen Northern
Joy O'Connor
Rosemary O'Daniel
Jennifer Offerman
Lynn Ogle
Kimberly Ossenberg
Mary Beth Ozete
Joan Paschen
Sandy Perry
Michelle Peterlin
Susan Pfender

RSTUVWYZ

Blythe Reherman
Marcia Rhodes
Hannah Rodocker
Melodie Roedel
Judy Rohleder
Vicki Rohleder
Billie Rose
Janie Royalty
Sharon Ruder
Tricia Ryan
Amy Samm
Nancy Sax
Patricia Schitter
Margy Schnakenburg

Claudia Schreiber
Jennifer Schultheis
Jodi Schwartz
Joann Schwentker
Monica Shakun
Julie Shoulders
Missy Singer
Jana Sly
Charleen Spear
Ellen Spence
Stasia Spentzas
Karyn Staples
Tiffany Stepto
Linda Stocks
Laura Stoltz
Deena Stovall
Janice Stover
Patricia Tharp
RaeAnn Titzer
Nancy Traylor
Niki Traylor
Jackie VanDelden
Shannon Vincek
Kelly Vogt
Kirsten Wagmeister
Melissa Wagner
Julie Ann Walker
Ann Waling
Sarah Warren
Crunchy Wells
Amy Welp
Lauren Whitledge
Jamie Wicks
Lynda Wilhelmus
Amy Will
Suzan Williams
Karlena Winiger
Susan Worthington
Diana Zausch
Patricia Ziemer

Recipe Testers

ABCDEFG

Kellie Adler
Lea Alcock
Brenda Aldridge
Kristie Alexander
Kristie M. Alexander
Peggy Annakin
Dawn Armeni
Ann Arosteguy
Noelle Barsumian
Cindy Behrens
Lisa Bindley
Jennifer Blackburn
April Boeke
Kari Bozarth
Shannon Brasseale
Suzette Broshears
Francesca Brougham
Hope Carroll
Barbara Compton
Suzie Consoer
Angie Cooley
Amanda Eagleston
Jane Elgin
Ann Enlow
Amy Fluck
Shawna Forte
Heather Gardner
Melissa Gillenwater
Sharon Gonzales
Lori Goris
Mindy Graper

HIJKL

Stacy Haertel
Shara Hammet
Wendy Hanafee
Kimberly Haywood-Pfender
Allison Hemmerlein
Bethany Hunt
Toscha Hurm
Linda Johnson
Nikki Keith
Janet Keller
Heather Kent
Sonya Kincaid
Linda Kinkel
Michele Kinkel
Ellen Kirkpatrick
Nancy Koehler
Amy Kolleck
JoAnne Kotmel
Dana Lewis
Crystal Loudermilk
Allison Lueking
Joelle Lynch

MNOPQR

Jennifer Mann
Wendy McCormick
Debbie McDaniel
Kathy McMurray
Karen Meacham
Rachael Miles
Andrea Miller
Sara Miller
Kimberly Moman
Lori Moore
Lynn Muehlbauer
Jamie Neel
Karen Northern
Joy O'Connor
DeLoris Ogle
Lynn Ogle
Mary Beth Ozete
Imogene Parker
Joan Paschen
Sandy Perry
Michelle Peterlin
Susan Reid
Lisa Reising
Melissa Robinson
Hannah Rodocker
Vicki Rohleder
Billie Rose
Janie Royalty
Tricia Ryan

STUVWXYZ

Amy Samm
Patricia Schitter
Margy Schnakenburg
Jennifer Schultheis
Monica Shakun
Julie Shoulders
Missy Singer
Jana Sly
Stasia Spentzas
Karyn Staples
Tiffany Stepto
Linda Stocks
Kate Stumpf
Lori Tang
Erika Taylor
RaeAnn Titzer
Jill Trautvetter
Niki Traylor
Jan Vanderhuitgaren
Elizabeth Verkamp
Kirsten Wagmeister
Melissa Wagner
Julie Ann Walker
Melanie Walsh
Amy Welp
Starla West
Jamie Wicks
Amy Will
Andrea Wittmer
Diana Zausch

200

We sincerely apologize if we have inadvertently omitted a name.
We are grateful to all who made this book and its contents possible.

Sidebar Contributors

ABCDEF

Lea Alcock
Dawn Armeni
Ann Arosteguy
Suzette Broshears
Francesca Brougham
Jean Brubeck
Allison Comstock
Billie Dees
Ann Enlow
Terrence Friedman

GHIJKL

Kimberly Haywood-Pfender
Alison M. Hemmerlein
Janet Keller
Michelle Kerr Heuck
Heather King
Michele Kinkel
Amy Kolleck

MNOPQR

Maxine's Café and Bakery
Karen Meacham
Andi Miller
MOKAZ
Stephanie Morris
Karen Northern
Thomas O'Connor
Lynn Ogle
Kim Ossenberg
Michelle Peterlin
Susan Reid

STUVWXYZ

Mike and Shelly Sackett
Darby Schnakenburg
Luise F. Schnakenburg
Melissa Singer
Ellen Spence
Karen Staples
Kate Stumpf
Erika Taylor
Tomelle Tornatta
Niki Traylor
Kristen Tucker
Shannon Vincek
Kirsten Wagmeister
Melissa Wagner
Julie Ann Walker
Carrie Webb-McCune

Index

202

Index

Index

Index

Index

Once Upon a Time

The Junior League of Evansville, Inc.
123 Northwest Fourth Street
Suite 422
Evansville, Indiana 47708
812-423-9127
www.juniorleagueofevansville.com

Name _____

Street Address _____

City _____ State _____ Zip _____

Telephone _____ Email Address _____

YOUR ORDER	QUANTITY	TOTAL
Once Upon a Time at $24.95 per book		$
Indiana residents add 6% sales tax		$
Postage and handling at $5.00 per book		$
TOTAL		$

Payment: [   ] MasterCard   [   ] VISA

[   ] Check enclosed payable to The Junior League of Evansville, Inc.

Account Number _____ Expiration Date _____

Signature _____

Where would you like to see copies of this book sold?

Store Name _____

Street Address _____

City _____ State _____ Zip _____

Photocopies will be accepted.